Regulatory Reform, Privatisation and Competition Policy

ORGANISATION FOR ECONOMIC CO-OPERATION AND DEVELOPMENT

ORGANISATION FOR ECONOMIC CO-OPERATION AND DEVELOPMENT

Pursuant to Article 1 of the Convention signed in Paris on 14th December 1960, and which came into force on 30th September 1961, the Organisation for Economic Co-operation and Development (OECD) shall promote policies designed:

— to achieve the highest sustainable economic growth and employment and a rising standard of living in Member countries, while maintaining financial stability, and thus to contribute to the development of the world economy;

— to contribute to sound economic expansion in Member as well as non-member countries in the process of economic development; and

— to contribute to the expansion of world trade on a multilateral, non-discriminatory basis in accordance with international obligations.

The original Member countries of the OECD are Austria, Belgium, Canada, Denmark, France, Germany, Greece, Iceland, Ireland, Italy, Luxembourg, the Netherlands, Norway, Portugal, Spain, Sweden, Switzerland, Turkey, the United Kingdom and the United States. The following countries became Members subsequently through accession at the dates indicated hereafter: Japan (28th April 1964), Finland (28th January 1969), Australia (7th June 1971) and New Zealand (29th May 1973). The Commission of the European Communities takes part in the work of the OECD (Article 13 of the OECD Convention). Yugoslavia has a special status at OECD (agreement of 28th October 1961).

Publié en français sous le titre :
RÉFORME RÉGLEMENTAIRE,
PRIVATISATION ET POLITIQUE DE LA CONCURRENCE

Foreword

This report on regulatory reform, privatisation and competition policy has been prepared by the OECD Secretariat for the Committee on Competition Law and Policy. It was approved by the Committee in June 1990 subject to some updating country amendments which have since been incorporated in the text. It generally reflects the situation as at the end of 1990.

The report is in two parts. Part I comprises a synthesis of work done earlier by the Committee, analysing the background to regulation and the reasons for reform, the extent and effect of deregulation as well as drawing some conclusions and making some suggestions for action for the consideration of OECD Member countries. Part II provides details on a country-by-country basis of the regulatory reforms and privatisation measures that have been put into effect or envisaged in the near future.

The OECD Council agreed to the derestriction of the report on 31 July 1991.

ALSO AVAILABLE

Agriculture and the Consumer (1990)
(24 90 02 1) ISBN 92-64-13411-5   FF65   £8.00   US$14.00   DM25

Competition Policy and the Deregulation of Road Transport (1990)
(24 90 03 1) ISBN 92-64-13428-X   FF75   £9.00   US$16.00   DM30

Competition Policy in OECD Countries

   1988-1989 (1991)
   (24 90 04 1) ISBN 92-64-13447-6   FF180   £22.00   US$38.00   DM70

Deregulation and Airline Competition (1988)
(24 88 02 1) ISBN 92-64-13101-9   FF100   £12.00   US$22.00   DM43

Contents

Part I

Synthesis Report

Introduction — Scope and Objectives of the Report

Since the mid-1970s, a number of OECD countries have undertaken substantial regulatory reform. Regulation has been removed from areas of the economy in which it had previously been rigorously applied, while in areas where regulation remains appropriate, the methods of regulation have been re-assessed. The process of regulatory reform has been most actively pursued in New Zealand, the UK and the US, but has been undertaken, or actively considered, to varying degrees in all Member countries. These developments are in line with an OECD Council Recommendation of 1979[1] which followed from a report on competition policy in regulated sectors.[2]

This report provides an analysis of the regulatory reforms of member nations, assessing the extent and effect of these changes, and drawing lessons for future competition policy. Section 2 begins by outlining the main economic reasons for government regulation — combating market failure in a variety of forms — and describing the methods of regulation most commonly employed. Section 3 focuses on the reasons why these regulations have been found wanting, notably the growing experience of regulatory failure and the changing nature of the industry under regulation.

Section 4 summarises the varying types of regulatory reform, including privatisation, which have occurred (more details on these will be found in Part II of the Report). Section 5 then examines the main effects of the reforms on the performance of the now deregulated sectors, noting the important influence of competitive pressures, before outlining the competition policy implications in Section 6. This section highlights circumstances in which complete deregulation is appropriate, opportunities for improving regulation, and the possible benefits and disadvantages of a variety of regulatory arrangements — stressing both the need in many cases to find a balance between market failure and regulatory failure, and for any solution to encourage rather than discourage market forces. Finally, Section 7 draws a number of conclusions for competition policy and makes some suggestions for action.

Introduction — Scope and Objectives of the Report

Section 2

The Reasons for Regulation and Public Ownership, and Methods of Regulation

A. Rationale for Regulation

A major justification of government intervention in the economy, through either legislation or expenditure, is the view that consumer welfare will not be maximised in all circumstances by leaving private sector firms to pursue their individual profit-maximising strategies and that the costs of government intervention are likely to be offset by the benefits.

Competitive markets will, under certain conditions, secure the efficient allocation of resources. Product market competition causes firms to produce goods that meet consumers' requirements at prices which reflect the relative costs of supply. At the same time, only firms that minimise costs and develop an efficient mix of factor inputs are able to succeed, while those that do not will be vulnerable to takeover, if there is competition in capital markets.

When the above conditions do not apply, however, markets may fail. In such circumstances, governments frequently intervene through public ownership and/or other forms of regulation, intending to remedy the market failure.

Historically, regulation has been justified on a variety of non-economic grounds related to the public interest, such as the need to maintain a particular industry for reasons of national security or ensure a nationwide network of services or to protect and encourage the development of a new industry, or, in the case of banking and insurance, to maintain the prudential supervision of people's savings. In addition, regulation of entry, prices and profits of such industries as road haulage and airlines grew during the 1930s when it was thought that "excessive" or "destructive" competition would occur if unrestricted entry and price competition were allowed, resulting in price wars, bankruptcy and unemployment. This claim of instability was often advanced by the industry itself but seldom justified by the facts.

This report focuses on two broad types of market failure which can justify regulation on economic grounds: circumstances where competitive solutions do not exist (natural monopoly) and circumstances where they exist but are not efficient (because of externalities and information asymmetry). In each case, government intervention to remedy ("regulate") the failure may be appropriate. Each is discussed in turn, beginning with those markets in which competitive solutions do not appear to exist.

Natural monopoly arises when the least cost method of production is by a single plant or firm rather than by several plants or firms. If only one output is produced, a condition for natural monopoly is the existence of economies of scale. In the event that more than one output can be produced from the same plant, then a necessary condition is the existence of economies of scope (i.e. the cost of producing several outputs jointly is less than the cost of producing them separately). Natural monopolies are most common in industries with major distribution networks, which imply substantial fixed costs, such as gas, electricity, water, railways and, to a decreasing extent, telecommunications. Provision by a single supplier is the most efficient outcome in these sectors because it avoids wasteful duplication: competition, therefore, would appear entirely inimical to efficient production.

Potential competition can, however, exist even where there is natural monopoly. In certain circumstances, the threat of potential entry may produce a competitive solution, even though there is monopolistic supply. Such a market is described as "contestable"[3] in that entrants do not face disadvantages in relation to the incumbent monopolist in terms of sunk costs and scale of production. In practice, few regulated sectors appear to exhibit the characteristics that make a monopoly "contestable".

In most cases natural monopoly is not contestable, and profit maximisation is not consistent with the maximisation of consumer welfare or the public interest. For such a monopoly to persist requires that significant barriers prevent competitors from entering the market.

Externalities. The second area of market failure is where there is a competitive market, but this does not produce the most efficient solution for reasons other than economies of scale. The principal issues to be considered here are externalities, public goods and asymmetries of information. Externalities arise where the production or consumption of a commodity has effects which extend beyond those who are directly concerned with that production or consumption. The most commonly used example is pollution, whereby a producer imposes costs on the wider community that are not reflected in its own costs. This particular form of market failure has led to a host of government environmental or safety regulations or to the regulation of a number of particular industries (e.g. water).

Asymmetric Information. Competitive markets also require some degree of equality of information between consumers and suppliers. However, this equality is often absent, particularly when the good or service being provided has a large information content or is purchased infrequently. Thus, complex goods and legal and other specialist advice inevitably suffer from information asymmetry. It is the additional information possessed by the specialist that the consumer is purchasing; thus the consumer faces considerable difficulties in evaluating the quality of the information provided. The supplier may therefore be able to perform inefficiently yet not be penalised by loss of business. Reputation can alleviate some of these problems, increasing consumer awareness of supplier quality, and providing strong incentives to suppliers to improve or maintain quality. However, the establishment of a reputation is a lengthy and expensive process, and will never be an entirely satisfactory substitute for direct information about the quality of supply.[4] Again, there is a prima facie governmental role in remedying this particular market failure, particularly by requiring the provision of information by suppliers or facilitating an independent market for information to purchasers.

B. Different Methods of Government Regulation

At a general economy-wide level *competition legislation* can remedy or prevent uncompetitive corporate structures, monopolistic price setting or cartel behaviour which prevent competition from working where there is no reason why there should be a persistent market failure. Governments have traditionally responded to more lasting forms of market failure with regulation. "Regulation" encompasses both structural regulation — concerned with the structure of an industry — and conduct regulation — concerned with the behaviour of those within an industry (although the distinction between the two is often blurred). Regulation can be applied through a variety of regulatory instruments. Price or profit regulation may be required to remedy a particular market failure or if the market failure results from a natural monopoly, regulators have often taken the view that public ownership is the appropriate response. This section provides an overview and evaluation of the various forms of regulation, beginning with structural regulation, then conduct regulation and ending with public ownership. Another type of regulation — the regulation of standards — may also be used by governments to constrain the behaviour of firms (e.g. health, safety or pollution standards). However, this lies beyond the scope of this paper which is concerned solely with economic regulation, that is the process by which government issues instructions which alter the resource allocation decisions by economic agents.

Structural regulation takes place when the regulatory authority determines which firms are allowed or required to engage in particular activities. It seeks to rule out business options that may be desirable from the company's perspective, e.g. entry into another industry, but which are undesirable from a public interest viewpoint and which are difficult to regulate by conduct control. Thus, in order to prevent excess capacity in certain sectors regulations have been introduced to control entry, e.g. by limiting the number of licences awarded to firms to operate in the industry. Likewise, exit regulation can ensure that a company does not withdraw from activities that have a social benefit but are inefficient from the company's viewpoint. Structural regulation has thus often been used to provide a broad range of services, including those regarded as socially necessary but unprofitable. The government-created monopolist, protected from entry, has been encouraged to internally cross-subsidise products and services to meet these requirements. The inefficiency which this entails has been recognised. For example, direct subsidy rather than cross-subsidisation is being increasingly used for the provision of uneconomic bus services, allied with the introduction of competitive tendering for such services.

Conduct Regulation. Whilst European governments until recently tended to focus on the direct regulation of prices through ownership, US governments attempted to direct the behaviour of monopolies by focussing on particular aspects of their conduct. The most common approach was to require monopolies to carry out their activities without earning the "abnormal" profits that normally follow monopolistic production. This was attempted directly, by the regulator placing compulsory limits on the amount of profit companies are permitted to earn. In setting this limit, the regulator had to tackle two issues — determining what constitutes an efficient level of performance and devising incentives to ensure its achievement.

In its simplest form, US regulators approached these tasks by putting a ceiling on the rate of return on assets. However, despite its directness, this method suffers from a number of difficulties. Most importantly, it allows increases in costs above efficient levels to be

13

passed on to the customer through higher prices. Conversely there is no extra profit in reducing inefficiencies and seeking out more effective technologies. The consequence is that the rewards and incentives usually associated with private ownership are effectively negated. Indeed, such regulation can also convey adverse incentives. Over-capitalization is encouraged[5] as are distortions in the pricing structure in favour of capital-intensive outputs because the monopoly has the incentive to maximise the total revenue it can extract for any given rate of return.

The switch in UK regulatory policy from public ownership to profit/price control in the 1980s sought to improve on the US approach. The method finally adopted in the UK was first recommended by Professor Littlechild in a report commissioned by the Government on the regulation of the privatised British Telecom.[6] It has become known as RPI-X (RPI minus X) regulation and has been adopted in the case of telecommunications, gas and airports. In France, a similar method was applied in the 1980s, for example to the railways (SNCF), France Télécom and Electricité de France. Some similar regulation — "price caps" — has recently been introduced in the US, notably in telecommunications.

Although the detail of the individual regulatory arrangements is complex, the underlying principles are relatively straightforward. A ceiling is put on the annual increase in the enterprise's prices — the ceiling being established at X percentage points below the increase in the Retail Price Index. X was fixed at 3 for British Telecom for the first five years following privatisation (for four years from 1989 it is 4.5) and 1 for British Airports Authority. For British Gas, X was fixed at 2 for the first five years after privatisation, though a modified formula allows it to pass on changes in the cost of its energy supplies. The Office of Gas Supply is about to embark on a review of the tariff price formula.

If the company subject to price ceilings reduces its costs by more than the amount assumed in the (RPI - X) calculation, it is rewarded by earning benefits in the form of higher profits. Conversely, if costs are reduced by less than that presumed in the formula, the enterprise suffers reduced profitability.

The incentives inherent in (RPI-X) regulation are clearly very different from those arising from the direct regulation of profit. A profit-maximizing enterprise regulated by (RPI-X) is strongly encouraged to achieve productive efficiency. However, the practical effect of these different incentives may not be as significant as might be argued, particularly where shareholders are not able to exercise sufficient control over the performance of their company.

The effectiveness of the (RPI-X) formula will therefore depend on whether or not the regulator can determine what constitutes an efficient level of performance, and then structure the formulas in such a way that a failure to achieve efficient performance will be reflected in the basic financial indicators which prompt shareholder action. In this respect, there may be some doubt as to whether the regulator is any better placed than the shareholders. Like the shareholder, the regulator needs information upon which to base an assessment of performance. Unless, however, this assessment is substantially independent of the enterprise's achieved level of costs and efficiency, (RPI-X) regulation will become equivalent, in practice, to rate-of-return regulation, with all its associated weaknesses.[7] Furthermore, the regulator may still be vulnerable to capital-intensive companies manipulating short-term performance in order to escape the regulatory constraints.

Public Ownership. Public ownership has been a widely utilised instrument of regulatory intervention, particularly in the European economies. The term "public owner-ship" usually refers to government funded activities that are commercial, industrial or financial, and in which economic goods or services are directly produced and "sold" to the consumer (although monetary exchanges need not always take place). The precise form of public ownership has varied considerably, both between and within nations, and over time within a particular industry. Public enterprises have ranged from organisations operating within government structures as part of a ministry, to publicly-quoted joint-stock companies in which government is a largely passive majority shareholder.

The rationale for public ownership stems from a simple view of the relationship between ownership and control. Privately owned companies are held to be profit maximisers, as by maximising profits they maximise the benefits to shareholders alone. In some cases, maximising shareholder benefits does not maximise benefits to society as a whole. Thus, public ownership, by replacing the narrow interests of the shareholders with the wider interests embodied in the state, will cause the company to abandon profit maximisation and pursue instead that mixture of profit and other factors that maximises social, as opposed to private, benefits. Evidently, this is chiefly a rationale for nationalisation of an entire industry. Publicly owned enterprises operating in a commercial environment cannot be made subject to these profit constraints.

The mechanism by which ownership change was to bring about such changes in company behaviour is nowhere precisely defined. Public ownership may secure "the commanding heights of the economy",[8] but the chain of command is unclear. At best, there is a reliance on a change in the nature of senior management, the private sector profit seeker being replaced by the civil servant "high custodian of the public interest"[9] — though, in practice, the two have frequently been one and the same. Thus, private benefits continued to be pursued, although what was maximised often changed (Rees, for example, found that certain public enterprises maximised output).[10]

There are many examples of public ownership suffering from poorly defined, and often changed, objectives; and a loss of managerial responsibility and accountability — the relatively consistent oversight of the stock market having been replaced by the unpredict-able supervision of elected ministers.

Each of these methods of regulation has been employed within the OECD, both singly and in tandem, although their use has varied between and within nations, and over time. In recent years, however, the pattern of government intervention in the economy has altered across the OECD. There has been a movement away from public ownership towards privatisation, deregulation, and pro-competitive re-regulation with the industries involved being subject to the relevant competition law.

Section 3

Reasons for Change

Two key factors have underlain the changing approach of OECD governments towards regulation. The first is the growing awareness of the extent and nature of regulatory failure. The second is changes in technology and a better understanding of organisational structure and behaviour that have fundamentally altered the incidence of market failure. These two elements underpin the arguments at the heart of the recent micro-economic debate concerning the poor performance of the regulated (nationalised) sector, labour market rigidities, government financial needs, and wider share ownership.

Regulatory Failure. The experience of several decades of governmental regulation has led to a growing recognition that failure is not confined to markets — governments can also fail. Interventions intended to correct market failure can often have adverse, although unintended, consequences for the achievement of efficiency.

The traditional theory of regulation presupposed that if the objectives of the government regulatory authorities and the regulated enterprise were identical, then the possibility of regulatory failure was removed. Policy towards regulated industries has often been founded on this view of the objectives of public enterprise managers; policy-makers assumed that if the managers of state owned firms were told to pursue the public interest, they would be able to determine what that meant and would have the necessary incentive to implement it. In practice, the vagueness of the objectives and the difficulty of precisely determining a socially optimal output level, has proved inimical to the efficient management of the industries concerned. The objectives of the regulatory authority and the enterprise diverge. This divergence of objectives, typical of many regulated industries, can be characterised in a principal-agent framework.

The principal (the regulatory authority) relies upon an agent (the enterprise) to achieve its objectives in circumstances where their objectives diverge and their access to information is asymmetrical.[11] In these circumstances, the regulator will need information in order to regulate effectively. But the best (and, where there is monopoly, the only) source of that information is the regulated company — which has a strong incentive to supply inadequate or incorrect information, for example by overestimating its costs. In this way, the regulated firm tries to influence the regulator to its advantage and at the cost of distorting the allocation of resources.[12]

As noted in Chapter 2, regulation may be effected for a variety of public interest concerns, reasons unrelated to economic efficiency, such as the maintenance of particular services on social grounds. Such regulation will therefore almost by definition distort the price mechanism, leading to cross-subsidisation of the "uneconomic" activities. Hence a

17

number of regulated sectors have been characterised by excessive costs or too frequent services or too high quality standards in relation to what consumers are willing to pay for. These disbenefits underlie the motive for the considerable international momentum behind fundamental regulatory reform and deregulation.

Another argument for deregulation has been the re-appraisal of the "protectionist/ strategic industry" argument for regulation. Historically, many investment projects and jobs have been subsidised or legislated for by government to enable particular companies or industries to resist the pressures of market forces. This has often been justified by citing "market failure" of a general kind. Typically, a government will argue that it is in the "public interest" that there is, for example, a strong shipbuilding industry, which, in the particular case, market forces would fail to provide. Thus government should regulate to protect the industry and its jobs from market forces.

In practice, regulatory intervention of this kind has, in most cases, been unsuccessful. Market failure so broadly defined presents considerable problems when formulating industry or company specific policy — whether the problems confronting a given company or sector indicate serious market failure or the necessary costs of dynamic adjustment is often unclear until some time after policy decisions are taken. Thus, the success or failure of such policies is difficult to assess, and there is a danger that the government will become committed to preserving a company and its jobs whatever the cost. This may prevent more effective action to maximise wealth and employment — such as the transfer of labour and other resources to more profitable, growing sectors of the economy.

Greater consumer awareness of the services provided in other nations has frequently created dissatisfaction with relatively poor provision in domestic markets which have been protected from international competition. For example, the use of answer-phone machines in the US led British consumers to question why they had neither the opportunity to purchase a UK equivalent nor the ability to connect an imported machine into the British Telecom network. Their questions created considerable pressure for change.

Poor Performance of Regulated Sectors. The perception of poor performance in the regulated sectors is widespread across the OECD. This perception has been based generally on comparisons with deregulated sectors in other countries or in parts of the country which have been subject to deregulation. In the US one of the early pieces of evidence in favour of airline deregulation was the study of intrastate partially deregulated airlines in Texas and California which revealed considerably more price competition than that prevailing in interstate markets of comparable size and distance.[13] In the US, increases in the rate of regulation accounted for between a quarter and a half of the decline in total factor productivity between the early 1960s and mid-1970s.[14] Similarly, New Zealand's experience of 20 years of the lowest growth amongst high income nations is at least partly the result of government instituted barriers to trade and regulation of both the labour market and the behaviour of businesses in the service sector.[15]

Where the regulated sectors have been predominantly under public ownership, poor performance has also been observed.[16] However, this has frequently prompted the conclusion that the observed poor performance is primarily a consequence of state ownership, rather than the weak incentives to improve performance.

Some authors however have argued that public enterprises are particularly prone to inefficiency because of their control structure, which protects them against poor performance. In a private enterprise, internal control by shareholders and the threat of take-over externally provide incentives to efficiency which are not present in publicly owned enterprises.[17]

Regulation can provoke poor performance in a number of ways. Management can be or feel restrained by regulatory oversight — low salaries, political interference in decision making, and limitations on new business initiatives. In the late 1970s, senior management of Cable & Wireless in the UK resigned because of the low level and political determination of salaries, whilst the US business community rebelled against the cost and pervasiveness of regulation.[18] In Australia, the need for greater flexibility to compete against non-banking financial institutions led the regulated banks to seek the removal of regulations restricting their activities.[19]

Poor performance may also be precipitated, or made more likely, by regulatory change in other nations. The US deregulation of airlines enabled US carriers to charge substantial discounts on flights to and from Canada, thus subjecting the still-regulated Air Canada to considerable pressure. Although the Canadian national airline remained reluctant to forfeit its protected position, it was unable to persuade the government to resist the economic pressure to deregulate.

Labour Market Effects. Labour market problems have also had considerable impact on the movement to regulatory reform. The performance of public sectors which had been used to implement policies of covert employment subsidy — "the industry must be supported to protect jobs" — began to deteriorate as strong unions provoked both costly industrial action and pay rises in excess of any improvements in productivity. The consequences for both the specific sectors and the structure of the economy as a whole were sufficient to generate support for the reduction of such policies as employment subsidy — to the extent that, in the UK, for example, between 1979 and 1988, 341,000 workers (53 per cent of the total employed at the start of the period) were shed from British Coal, British Steel & British Rail alone.[20]

In Australia, it was the centralised regulation of wage negotiations, rather than employment subsidy, that came under attack — and it was the workers themselves that were the leading protagonists. The adverse conditions facing the Australian economy, combined with government macro-economic policies, reduced the real wages of much of the labour force, and prompted the labour movement to suggest changes in the system of wage regulation to allow the market more play.[21]

In New Zealand, labour relations legislation was amended to allow for some flexible bargaining structures.

There have been attempts, notably in the privatisation programmes of France, and in the UK, to improve the incentives of the labour force through the use of worker share ownership and management buyout schemes.

Budgetary Considerations. Regulatory reform presented governments with the prospect of significant budgetary benefits. Streamlining the regulatory machinery could bring substantial cost savings, whilst, through privatisation, capital assets could be exchanged for a direct cash injection into the public sector current account. As financial pressures on government mounted during the 1970s, the attraction of these potential benefits grew. These financial pressures on government included negative demands — alleviating financial crisis — and positive needs, such as capital investment in state industries. Thus, in Japan, rising government debt (up from 9.2 per cent of GDP in 1974 to 41.2 per cent in 1982) led to the appointment of the Provisional Commission for Administrative Reform in 1980 — a body that recommended a number of cost-saving reforms including privatisation, and paved the way, indirectly, to the deregulation of financial and other markets.[22] The Australian government's need for an effective monetary policy to tackle adverse economic conditions prompted the beginning of deregulation in the financial sector.[23] In France, the FF50 billion proceeds of the privatisations of 1986/7 went to repay public debts, and to capital investment in other publicly owned companies — including FF3 billion for Renault alone,[24] whilst in the UK, the twin priorities of investment and tight monetary policy produced the "flagship" privatisation of British Telecom.[25] Subsequent privatisations in the UK have contributed sizeable sums to the National Exchequer.

Similar stories can be told for other OECD nations. However, although they were at times extremely important, it would be wrong to conclude that budgetary considerations were an overriding motivation for regulatory reform. Governments always face financial pressures of varying degree. The changed perception of market failure, and the recognition that expensive regulatory apparatus was often far from efficient, allowed politicians to contemplate what, a decade previously, would have been unthinkable — that regulatory reform offered an additional means by which the government's financial needs could be met. This regulatory reform movement can also be explained as part of a wider appreciation throughout the 1980s of the advantages of the market provision of goods and services over their regulated provision, a reform which had begun to be extended to the countries of Eastern Europe by the end of the decade.

Wider Political Goals. Finally, there were a number of motivations for regulatory reform that were limited to particular countries. Both France and the United Kingdom sought to use privatisation to widen share ownership — with the intention, in the UK at least, of promoting the ideology of "popular capitalism".[26] The French privatisations also aimed to boost the developing Paris stock exchange.[27]

Reassessing Market Failure in the Light of Changing Technology. Regulatory intervention has been justified as a response to market failure. Market failure should not, however, be viewed as a static concept, fixed for all time. Rather, it is determined by technology, market conditions, and organisational structure. Thus, recent developments in technology have led to a reappraisal of the nature and extent of market failure in the economy.

The effect of changing technology is demonstrated most powerfully in the telecommunications industry. Until the development of digital networks and micro-wave transmission, the only opportunity for introducing competition lay in the installation of a cable network identical to that already established — a costly and inconvenient process for which there was no apparent demand. However, the increase in demand for services has enabled alternative networks to achieve the minimum efficient scale of operation and to compete effectively with the existing system, first for international, and then on trunk, calls.

Within a few years, it is possible that competition will take place at a local level, and some parts of the natural monopoly network will have been entirely superseded.[28] A similar story can be told in broadcasting, where monopolistic supply based on a natural transmission monopoly — the scarcity of available wavelengths — has been ended by the development of competitive cable and satellite broadcasting systems.

Technological change does not always operate to undermine natural monopoly, however. In some cases, such as airline reservation systems, technological developments may give rise to new natural monopolies due to the existence of significant economies of scale. However, at present, there are a number of airline reservation systems in operation which offer competitive choices to consumers.

Understanding the ways in which the various components of a company interact has improved considerably since the early attempts at regulation. Then, the existence of a natural monopoly activity within a business would lead the regulator to regard all operations of the company as a natural monopoly. However, many parts of such a business may be competitive — for example, electricity supply includes natural monopoly in transmission, potential competition in generation, and potential competition in the supply of user equipment. To treat these activities as if they were all natural monopolies would bring about considerable efficiency losses. Many of the regulatory changes in recent years reflect the attempt to unravel the competitive activities within a company from those that are natural monopolies, and to tailor policies accordingly.

The international development of improved technology in many industries (for example in telecommunications equipment or in electricity generation) has made protected national companies increasingly vulnerable to those firms that have updated their technology in response to market forces. The open-ended protection of national producers from international competitors has thus often been misplaced; by cushioning companies from the need to adapt, protection has left them more vulnerable in the long term to international competition.

The impact of the globalisation of markets has also extended to countries where protectionism has brought success at a macro level. Such nations have been subjected to considerable pressure from the international community to change policies as foreign competitors have demanded, often with the backing of trade sanctions, the ending of protectionist regulation and a better functioning international market.

Various Types of Regulatory Reform and Privatisation in OECD Member Countries

Regulatory reform is understood in this section in a very broad sense to cover not only the removal or reform of regulations on price, entry, exit, output or services but also the relaxation of private or public monopolies and the withdrawal of exemption from competition laws (i.e. by extending such laws to encompass sectors previously immune).

The pattern and speed of regulatory reform have been uneven in OECD countries, although one can discern similar preoccupations in some industries which have been subject to differing degrees of regulation in the first place. This chapter surveys the changes that have occurred by comparing and contrasting the regulatory reforms undertaken over the last ten years or so. While many different sectors have been involved, there are five broad industries which have been the particular object of attention in many countries. These are the energy sector (oil, gas and electricity), air, sea and road transport, posts and telecommunications, banking and financial services and radio and television broadcasting. For more details the reader is referred to Part II of this report, which includes the result of a survey of OECD Member countries on deregulation and privatisation in the transport, energy, posts and telecommunications sectors as well as details of regulatory reforms undertaken since this Committee's last report on the subject.

While it is generally agreed that the United States began the process of deregulation in the mid-1970s with far-reaching initiatives in several sectors such as airlines, trucking, railways and banking,[29] there were sporadic moves earlier in other countries. For example, road haulage was substantially deregulated in Australia, Sweden, Switzerland and the United Kingdom in the 1950s and 1960s. Generally speaking, however, it was the decade of the 1980s which ushered in the related processes of regulatory reform and, especially, privatisation.

Energy

The oil shocks of the 1970s initially led to increased intervention by governments in an attempt to control price increases and to assure supplies. Hence output, price and purchasing controls were widespread. In the easier supply conditions of the 1980s, these regulations were replaced by the gradual withdrawal of intervention in the oil and gas production sectors and moves to inject competition into the energy supply sector. The US deregulated oil prices between 1979 and 1982. Canada deregulated oil prices and lifted export controls in 1985 and deregulated natural gas markets in 1986. Proposals have also been put forward to separate the marketing and transportation functions of pipelines in Canada and to introduce brokerage in gas pipeline transportation in the United States. Several European countries have acted to abolish the State monopoly of refining and distribution, especially those European countries which are members of the EC. France lifted all controls over retail prices in 1985 and, in 1987, liberalised the conditions for the import of petroleum products. Finland abolished price control of oil products in 1988. In Australia, from January 1988 refiners and crude oil producers have been able to negotiate freely quantities and prices. The Government has also moved towards a free market for liquid petroleum gas. In New Zealand, also in 1988, the Government removed the main regulations relating to the distribution of motor spirit. By the end of the decade, few vestiges of price control remained.

The energy sector has also been marked by privatisation in several countries — the United Kingdom and Germany. In the United Kingdom, Britoil and Enterprise Oil were sold off in 1982 and 1984, respectively, and British Gas in 1986. The privatisation and splitting up of the electricity industry to introduce competition in generation and supply is also currently under way. In Germany, the sale of the Government's shareholding in VEBA and VIAG has led to the State withdrawing almost totally from ownership of the energy sector, although some Laender governments still have a stake in local electricity companies. In New Zealand the 1986 State-owned Enterprises Act and the 1987 State Enterprises Restructuring Act transformed the regulatory environment of State-owned enterprises, including the Electricity and Coal Corporations established under the former Act, and removed many of the statutory barriers to competition.

Transport

This sector has arguably been the one most subjected to regulatory reform. Although all transport modes have been affected, historically, road haulage was the first segment of the industry to be deregulated with four countries beginning the process in the 1950s and 60s — Australia, Switzerland, Sweden and the United Kingdom. During the 1980s many other OECD countries have followed suit, most of them in the last few years — Canada, Denmark, France, Japan, New Zealand, Norway, Portugal and the United States, and, in the European Communities, a certain degree of liberalisation has occurred in intra-Community road freight, although further progress remains to be made in the abolition of national quotas and the introduction of cabotage before one can speak of complete liberalisation in the EEC. In all these mentioned countries regulation of entry and prices has been abolished or substantially reduced. Some countries — Finland, Germany and Spain — have so far not proceeded very far down the road to deregulation.

Deregulation of passenger road transport has been less widespread; New Zealand, the United Kingdom and the United States have substantially deregulated long-distance or local buses. Australia has deregulated inter-provincial bus services but there remain intra-State regulations. Sweden has also recently abolished the public convenience and need test for a licence to operate passenger services.

The United Kingdom has recently not only deregulated bus services outside London but has also embarked on a process of privatisation and dismemberment of the formerly State-owned National Bus Company. The 1985 Act provided for the restructuring and sale of NBC's subsidiaries; 72 subsidiaries were created and sold between 1986 and 1988. (Subsequent mergers have created a number of larger groupings of ex-NBC companies.)

The railway industry has also not been subjected to much change, the notable exceptions being Japan and the United States. In 1987, the Japanese National Railways were split up into six passenger companies and one freight company which have all been privatised. In the United States, the Staggers Rail Act 1980 substantially deregulated the railway industry, withdrawing the antitrust immunity for the industry. Conrail was privatised in 1986. In the United Kingdom, the privatisation of British Rail is also under consideration for a future parliament, while a number of British Rail subsidiary activities have been privatised, including British Rail Hotels, Sealink Ferries and British Rail Engineering.

Air transport deregulation, while less widespread than road haulage deregulation, also occurred in several countries in the 1980s, taking their lead from the US, where since 1978 domestic routes have been deregulated. Since 1982 US airline markets have been open to all domestic carriers that are fit, willing and able to enter. Carriers have had complete flexibility since 1983 to set passenger fares and have free entry to all routes. As in all other OECD countries, however, there remain restrictions on the entry of foreign airlines into US domestic markets as well as on foreign investment in the sector. In 1981, Australia allowed competition between air freight carriers and several other countries have substantially deregulated this segment — Norway, Sweden. As regards passenger transport, in the United Kingdom there has been partial deregulation of domestic routes beginning in 1976. In Canada there has been significant deregulation since 1988, with total deregulation in Southern Canada based on a simple "fit, willing and able" test while in Northern Canada a reverse onus test applies, i.e. objectors to a new service must establish that it will lead to a significant decrease or instability in the level of service. In New Zealand, over the period 1986 to 1988 restrictions on foreign ownership of domestic New Zealand airlines were progressively removed and changes were made to the regulatory regime intended to allow greater commercial flexibility. Australia has also announced that its long-standing two airline policy — under which air traffic on major domestic routes is reserved for two airlines — will end in 1990. The first phase of the EEC's programme of liberalisation of European air transport came into operation in 1988 which allows greater competition on capacity, routes and fares and the Council is committed to adopting further liberalisation by June 1990.

In addition to deregulation, four countries — Canada, Japan, New Zealand and the United Kingdom — have privatised national airlines, Air Canada, Japan Air Lines, Air New Zealand and British Airways, respectively, while in Germany, the government in 1989 reduced its shareholding in Lufthansa. In the United Kingdom, the British Airports Authority, which owns and operates seven international airports, was also privatised in 1987.

Some liberalisation has also occurred in Austria, France, and Portugal.

In 1987, two countries reformed their regulations on overseas shipping — Australia and Canada — with the aim of increasing competition between carriers and narrowing the scope of exemption for certain shipping conference practices. The EEC Council in 1986 adopted four regulations to apply the rules of competition to maritime transport and to ensure greater competition between carriers by preventing anticompetitive and unfair practices.

Posts and Telecommunications

Throughout the 1980s several OECD countries have pursued policies to separate the functions of the postal and telecommunications services, often as a first step towards deregulation and privatisation, at least of the telecommunications sector, but to some extent in the postal sector too, where some competition has been allowed from private operators to provide certain special letter and parcel delivery services.

The separation of the two activities has taken place in the United Kingdom (1981), Ireland (1984), New Zealand (1986) and Germany (1989). In Sweden, the two activities have traditionally been separated.

Three countries have privatised the national monopoly provider of telecommunications services — the United Kingdom (1984), Japan (1985) and New Zealand (1990) — at the same time as proceeding to substantial regulatory reform.

In the United Kingdom, following privatisation, a new regulatory authority OFTEL was set up to promote competition and to regulate the prices of British Telecom according to the RPI-X price formula. One new licence was issued to Mercury Communications, to compete against British Telecom. A more liberal licensing policy was pursued in relation to VANS and many operators have entered these markets.

In Japan, regulatory reform has in some ways gone significantly further than the United Kingdom with competition being introduced into all segments of the Japanese telecommunications market. At the end of 1988 the number of companies which had entered type I business (providing services over their own installed circuits) was 45 while the number which had entered type II business (offering services using lines installed by type I companies) amounted to 693.

It is however arguable that the US has gone further than either Japan or the United Kingdom, for in 1984, the vertically integrated monopoly supplier — AT & T — was broken up into eight operating companies, seven to supply local services while the eighth supplies long-distance services and includes the equipment manufacturer and research laboratories. The deregulation also allowed the resale of common carrier services and the withdrawal of the restriction on AT & T's entry to related fields. The policy of allowing free entry operating since 1976 has meant that considerable new entry took place, thus ensuring effective competition in the long-distance market.

It should be noted that many OECD countries have liberalised and deregulated the equipment sector and value added network services, even where the basic services remain subject to controls. The countries involved are Australia, Austria, Belgium, Canada, Denmark, Finland, France, Germany, Ireland, New Zealand, Portugal, the Netherlands, Norway, Spain, Sweden and the United Kingdom, while in 1988 the EEC Commission adopted a directive designed to open up the EEC market for telecommunications terminal equipment which has tended to be partitioned on national lines.

Financial Services

Regulatory reform in financial services has also been widespread. This has ranged from the abolition of interest rate controls in the US (1980), New Zealand (1984), Australia and Finland (both 1986), Spain (1987), Austria (1989) to the deregulation of the US (1976) and UK (1986) stock exchanges, substantial reform of the French Stock Exchange (1988) and the partial or complete removal in many countries of structural boundaries between different types of financial institution, allowing them to compete against each other. In the UK, the Building Societies Act of 1986 allowed much greater freedom for building societies to compete against banks in providing banking services. In Spain, savings banks were allowed to carry out some of the operations of banks in 1977, and similar changes have taken place in France (1978), Portugal (1981), and Australia (1984).

Privatisation of publicly owned financial institutions has taken place, or is being actively considered, in France (Société Générale, Paribas, Banque Indosuez), Germany (Deutsche-Verkehrs-Kredit-Bank), New Zealand (Bank of New Zealand, POSB) and the UK (National Girobank). Foreign banks have been allowed to establish subsidiaries in Australia (1985), Norway (1985) and Sweden (1986). In Norway, foreign insurance companies were permitted to establish themselves in 1988. The overall ability of European national regulators to inhibit competition in this area will be reduced with the completion of the internal market, intended for 1992. Following intervention by the EEC Commission, restrictive agreements between banks have been abandoned in Belgium and Ireland while rules and regulations of several London Commodity Exchanges were amended in order to abolish fixed commission rates and certain restrictions on membership.

Regulation remains tight, however, in many countries. Denmark and Germany control premium (price) levels in their insurance industries. The new legislation in the UK (the 1986 Financial Services Act) represents a shift in the regulatory framework towards broader consumer protection safeguards as the basis of regulation.

Radio and Television Broadcasting

This sector has undergone considerable regulatory reform and privatisation in recent years, with a move away in many countries from the State monopoly operating in this area to a more broadly based broadcasting system including private operators. Thus in France in 1986 television broadcasting was opened up to private enterprise and one public channel was privatised. The liberalisation of radio broadcasting took place earlier. Many other countries have followed this process by allowing private radio and television stations to operate in competition with publicly owned stations. Australia has had both public sector and commercial broadcasting channels for many decades and commercial broadcasting is being reviewed to ensure that there is only the minimum regulation necessary to achieve government objectives. Recent developments in satellite and cable transmission would suggest that competition is bound to increase in television broadcasting.

Public Ownership

Despite extensive reforms including some privatisation, in 1990 public enterprise continues to dominate the postal, telecommunications and railway sectors in OECD countries and is strongly represented in electricity, gas and airlines.[30] As regards postal services no country has yet abolished the state monopoly of basic letter services but parcel and courrier services have been partially deregulated or privatised in most countries (see Part II, Tables 10 and 15). Basic local and long distance telephone services remain under public ownership in Australia, Austria, Denmark, Ireland, Norway, Spain, Switzerland, Sweden and Turkey and are privately owned in Canada (though in three provinces public monopolies exist), Japan, New Zealand, the United Kingdom and the United States (see Part II, Table 16). There is however a great deal more private sector involvement in the value added and equipment sectors of the market (see Part II, Table 17).

In the energy industries, public ownership is widespread in electricity and gas generation, transmission and distribution with Australia, Austria, Denmark, Ireland, New Zealand, Norway (for electricity transmission and distribution), Spain (high voltage network), Sweden (transmission) and the United Kingdom (electricity) having State monopolies. However, in the United Kingdom, the electricity industry (with the exception of the nuclear capacity) will soon be privatised, while in New Zealand, the distribution sector of the electricity industry will be significantly liberalised and privatised. In Canada, the electricity industry is a provincial state monopoly. In Australia, there is no federal regulation of the gas industry but the vast majority of generating/transmission and distribution in each State or Territory is publicly owned. As regards the petroleum industry there is significantly more private ownership, only Finland and Ireland having total public ownership of production and Turkey of transportation (see Part II, Tables 4-6).

In the various transport modes, trucking appears to be the sector where there is the least amount of public ownership. By 1990 only Norway and Sweden had some public enterprises in this sector. Airlines show a significant trend towards more private ownership during the period 1975 to 1990 (see Part II, Table 9). In Australia and Canada, local buses are usually municipally owned and in many other countries there is a significant amount of local public ownership. In the United Kingdom, a number of municipally owned bus companies continue to exist, especially in London and Northern Ireland.

The Effects of Regulatory Reform on Performance

As noted in Section 4, the regulatory reforms of the last decade have taken a number of different forms. This chapter examines the effects of these reforms. However, measuring them is a far from simple task, and the analysis employs a variety of data. In particular, there are numerous industry or economy-wide factors that influence performance, that may enhance or hinder specific attempts at reform, and so cloud the results. Where there has been deregulation, we are primarily concerned with the effects on price, choice and entry. Where a publicly owned company operating in a competitive market has been privatised, profitability provides the best indicator of the results of removing regulatory interference, and where there is a combination of privatisation, deregulation and monopoly, the indicators range from profits to price via product quality and total factor productivity. Our analysis is, therefore, primarily concerned with the interaction between different ownership and regulatory regimes, and not with ownership change per se.

There have been numerous studies of ownership effects on performance, which together present a complex picture. Some studies show superior performance by public enterprises,[31] whilst others suggest that private enterprises do better. This conflicting picture is confirmed by the different conclusions reached in the major surveys of research in this area. Borcherding et al,[32] for example, conclude that the empirical findings are "consistent with the notion that public firms have higher unit cost structures", whilst Millward[33] finds "no broad support for private enterprise superiority".

The most important reason for this diversity in empirical evidence is the varying interaction between ownership and competition and the effects of regulation in markets where competition is absent. This leads us away from simple assertions about the supremacy of one kind of ownership over another towards a number of broad conclusions.

Where product markets are competitive, public and private enterprises perform more efficiently than when competition is absent. Thus, where there has been effective deregulation, there have been efficiency gains. Almost all evidence concerning deregulation supports this view. The deregulation of US aviation[34] brought lower prices on longer routes (although prices have increased on short relative to longer flights), and the development of the more efficient "hub and spoke" route network. If one takes into account increased flight frequencies as well as fare decreases the benefits seem overwhelmingly positive. Morrison and Winston have estimated that benefits to consumers have been of the order of $5.7 billion annually which have been distributed over all except the least dense, short distance markets.[35] The deregulation of aviation in New Zealand,[36] led to an 18 per cent increase in traffic on regular services in the first year.

The liberalisation of the air routes between Britain and the Netherlands also appears to have led to falling prices and increased traffic.[37] In Canada, greater market concentration has followed deregulation, with many of the smaller airlines being taken over by the two major airlines. Nevertheless, the cost of air travel in Canada overall has fallen.

In the UK, competition in sectors such as express coach services, telecoms apparatus, and domestic air services has widened choice and, to varying extents, cut prices. New entry has occurred on a number of domestic air routes, and new routes have been established in long-distance express coaching.[38] For some time after deregulation a considerable reduction in coach fares, of up to 40 per cent, occurred which increased competitive pressure on British Rail to improve its service and restructure fares, even though coach fares subsequently rose again.[39] As regards road haulage which several OECD countries have progressively deregulated over a period of 20 years or more, the positive results have clearly outweighed any disbenefits. Typically, following deregulation there have been an influx of new entrants, a fall in rates, an increased level of services and increases in employment.[40]

Moore[41] found that empty miles of truck haulage in the deregulated UK trucking industry was 34 per cent, compared with 45 per cent in the tightly regulated West German industry. Profits in the UK were significantly higher than in West Germany, whilst at the same time UK prices were lower. In France, the liberalisation of the quota system for road hauliers in 1986 had an immediate impact on lowering prices for both short-haul and long-haul freight. The switch to quality rather than quantity regulation of trucking in New Zealand has cut freight rates and reduced operating costs. Competition following deregulation has kept fares low in the Norwegian road freight transport industry.[42] The partial deregulation of trucking in 1980 in the United States has brought considerable benefits due to the relaxation of entry restrictions and changes in operating conditions. A recent study has concluded that average annual logistics cost savings were $38 billion from 1981 to 1986.[43]

In the first year after the deregulation and privatisation of the Japanese National Railway, passengers carried and passengers per kilometer increased across the companies concerned; after many years of losses, all the privatised firms moved into profit, and their long-term debts were substantially reduced.[44]

The deregulation and privatisation of local bus services in the United Kingdom outside London and Northern Ireland, which took effect from October 1986, has produced encouraging results, notably increased bus mileage, substantial savings in subsidies, the entry of many new private operators and the innovatory introduction of minibuses on many services. As regards fares, these have increased in most areas broadly in line with inflation. Real wages have fallen in the industry.

The deregulation of telecommunications services has generally prompted increased entry, and brought consumer benefits through lower prices. The range of services provided has also increased. In the US, the price of long-distance calls (likewise in Japan and the UK) has fallen; and the number of companies supplying long distance telephone services had increased services from 1 in 1970 to 400 in 1984.[45] In Japan, the deregulation and privatisation of 1985 has been followed by many new entrants into the industry. At the end of 1988 there had been 45 new entrants into type I business and 693 new entrants into type II business.[46] UK deregulation of telecommunications equipment has similarly been followed by a decline in real prices and a liberal policy towards value added networks has been pursued. By 1987 over 200 operators were able to offer some 800 value added services ranging from videotex and conference calls to electronic mail and retrieval systems. With regard to apparatus, some 8,500 items of subscriber terminal equipment had been approved for general use by end 1988.[47]

Where product markets are competitive, the performance of the publicly owned enterprise may match that of privately owned rivals. In Canada, the publicly owned Canadian National Railroad faced competition both from the privately owned Canadian Pacific and from alternative transport modes. Investigation of their performance has shown no difference in efficiency between the two railroad companies.[48]

Nevertheless, publicly owned companies in competitive markets may be hindered by regulatory constraints — and it is pertinent that some of the most successful UK privatisations have been of companies operating in competitive sectors — Cable & Wireless, Amersham International, Jaguar and National Freight Consortium,[49] where management seems to have taken advantage of the greater freedom and incentives available in the private sector.

In the UK, deregulation in the form of competitive tendering for services such as refuse collection and hospital cleaning has resulted in significant cost savings. However, the public sector suppliers have been able to win contracts by matching the efficiency of private sector competitors.[50] The more important influence on performance is competition rather than ownership.

In a number of cases, however, the results of deregulation have been more problematic. New entry has not always occurred at the level expected given the assumed contestability of the market and incumbent suppliers have not always found their position eroded by competition from new entrants. This has sometimes been the experience in the cases of airlines and long-distance coaches. Mergers following deregulation have also sometimes reduced the benefits that might otherwise have been expected.[51]

In other cases, partial deregulation has left significant parts of an industry uncompetitive, even though the deregulated segments have invariably brought increased competition and improved performance. Thus, the deregulation of telecommunications equipment and value added services has generally led to lower prices and improved consumer choice. However because of the danger of abuse of market power in basic telephone services, prices continue to be regulated for such services (Canada and UK) or closely monitored as in Japan. Likewise in air transport, deregulation of fares has occurred in some domestic markets, notably in the United States and the United Kingdom, but has not been widely extended to international air services. Some liberalisation of fares has however taken place in the European Communities.

In financial services, consumers now face greatly increased choice in banking services. However, anti-competitive practices by the financial institutions (including non-itemised charges, and financial penalties for account closure) are observed with increasing frequency.[52] Considerable potential gains from deregulation have been identified,[53] arising particularly from international competition eliminating the considerable price differentials between nations. However, there are significant difficulties in direct entry into national financial markets, and financial institutions appear instead to be focussing on entry by acquisition. Deutsche Bank has purchased Banca d'America e d'Italia, for example, and

Allianz, Germany's largest insurance company, has purchased Cornhill Insurance (UK), and RAS (Italy's second largest insurance company). This trend, if continued, may lead to much of the potential gains of competition being internalised in the financial institutions rather than passed on to the consumer.[54]

The importance of organisational and ownership structure on performance should not be underestimated, however. Even in competitive markets, there are examples of companies performing poorly over time. The retailing outlets operated by the (then) public sector gas and electricity enterprises have been consistently outperformed by similar privately owned retailers.[55] The publicly owned National Freight Corporation (NFC) was only able to remain in the highly competitive road haulage industry at the expense of continuing losses. The same was true of the (then) publicly owned Sealink Ferries. In the private sector, too, P & O Ferries operated loss-making services in the competitive cross-channel market for several years before reorganising their activities in the face of a threatened hostile takeover.

In each of these examples, the activity in question formed a very small part of the operations of a far larger public or private enterprise. The financial losses required to retain market share in the face of more efficient competitors were therefore not significant to the enterprises' overall financial health. This suggests that divestment of these activities from their parent enterprise would bring about improved performance (or exit from the market) — a conclusion that is confirmed in the cases of NFC and Sealink.

Where product market competition is absent, or partial, a more complex picture emerges. Studies of sectors as diverse as electric utilities in North America[56] and insurance services in West Germany[57] show no general support for the view that private firms are more efficient than public firms in these circumstances. In fact there is some indication that the regulation of private firms has distorted incentives in ways which has resulted in performance which falls short of corresponding public enterprises.

The partial deregulation of telecommunications and gas in the UK has also brought some mixed results. While the profitability of the privatised monopoly providers British Telecom (BT) and British Gas has improved following privatisation, criticism has been focussed on some aspects of the firms' behaviour. In the case of BT this led in July 1988 to further deregulation when Mercury began providing public call box services in competition with BT, requiring regulation of the terms on which access to the BT network would be granted. Also in 1988 British Gas' pricing policy towards industrial consumers was found to be against the public interest by the UK Monopolies and Mergers Commission which recommended inter alia that British Gas should publish a price schedule and not discriminate in pricing as well as that it should give greater transparency to common carriage terms and that it should not contract initially for more than 90 per cent of any new gas fields (the UK government has since set as a target that 10 per cent of new gas should be supplied to the market by suppliers other than British Gas).

Generally speaking, UK utilities which were publicly owned in 1979 and subsequently privatised have improved their efficiency over the last decade, particularly since 1983;[58] all the industries concerned have registered substantial productivity gains, and in most the improvement has been considerable.

Finally, it should be noted that two of the most frequently voiced fears about deregulation, that safety standards would fall and unemployment would rise, have not been borne out in those sectors for which information is available.

In terms of employment, experience in the United States with airline deregulation has generally been positive. Employment expanded in the industry following deregulation. Wages, however, were under downward pressure following the creation of low-cost competitors not bound by existing long-term labour agreements. In road transport, the search for efficiency has resulted in a reduction in real wages to drivers, but, again, employment seems to benefit. In the United States, drivers' wages were above the average industrial wage before deregulation but have since tended towards the average, suggesting that drivers were sharing in the rents created by entry restriction under regulation. Employment in the industry has generally increased or has declined less than the average for manufacturing industry during recession. In France, employment in the road transport sector increased by 20 000 from 1984 to 1987. Other countries report large numbers of new entrants following deregulation without providing specific statistics on increases in overall employment.

In terms of safety, the record is also positive. Countries which have begun economic deregulation in either the airline or road transport sector have uniformly maintained and improved existing safety regulations. Further, accident rates have nowhere increased following deregulation and in some cases have actually decreased, typically following a downward trend established prior to economic deregulation. In the airline sector, accident rates have decreased in the United States following deregulation in 1978. In road transport, the rate of fatal accidents involving heavy trucks decreased by one-third in the United States during the 1980s. Similarly in the United Kingdom, accident rates for both trucks and buses continue to fall following deregulation, with the improvement for trucks substantially greater than the improvement for private cars during the same period. Finally, the safety condition of trucks in the UK improved following deregulation, according to the failure rates in periodic vehicle inspections.

Section 6

The Role of Competition Policy

This report has examined the changes in regulatory intervention during the last decade; the underlying and immediate reasons for these changes; and, where possible, the effects of these changes on performance. This reveals that there have been marked — and sometimes dramatic — changes in the efficiency of many of the companies and industries concerned. The most positive results have occurred where regulatory reform has focussed on creating the conditions where effective competition can operate rather than on ownership change. This chapter sets out the implications of this analysis for competition policy, tackling the fundamental question: what is the appropriate role of competition policy in the economy? Here, "competition policy" is used in its broadest sense, encompassing all policy intended to promote competition in the economy, rather than the narrower use of the term as short-hand for general antitrust policy. Antitrust policy is embraced by the broader definition.

In addressing this question, it must be recognised that a variety of factors explain past government intervention. One of these was a response, however inadequate, to problems of market failure. Thus, if regulatory reform fails to remedy the market failure that initially prompted regulation, the simple removal or reduction of existing regulation is unlikely to bring about permanent benefits. The costs of the market failure will continue to be borne. Competition policy, then, should attempt to relieve market failure by methods that either avoid regulatory failure, or keep it to a minimum.

There are three main areas in which competition policy can play a positive reforming role: where a publicly owned enterprise is operating in a competitive product market; where product market competition is possible, but not yet achieved; and where there is no possibility of competition in the product market. The particular opportunities and problems in applying competition policy in each of these cases are discussed in turn. However, it should be emphasised that in all circumstances, the aim of competition policy should be the creation of conditions approximating as closely as possible to those generating effective and efficient private markets: relatively specific objectives; a clearer framework of constraints; and the pressures of competition.

Competitive Markets. There is no reason why the state should be able to run hotels or laundries, build cars, or deliver freight, more efficiently than the private sector. However, in the public sector, such activities may suffer from being subject to constraints on their financing and organisation structures which were intended primarily for activities with little commercial application, or for which politicians were held responsible. Where such constraints do apply, the appropriate policy response would seem to be the privatisation of publicly owned enterprises operating in competitively structured markets.

35

Publicly-owned companies involved in international competition may suffer from being too closely identified with the government of a particular country. Political considerations may colour commercial decisions taken by international customers and competitors. Although such companies may benefit on occasion from political patronage, particularly in terms of contracts from national governments, in competitive markets companies will perform more efficiently where commercial considerations are paramount. It is in areas such as these that privatisation has enjoyed its most conspicuously successful results.[59]

Where market failure is more central, however, the issues concerning competition policy are less easily resolved. Section 2 identified three major sources of market failure — monopoly, externality, and information. In each of these cases conflict may arise between the underlying market failure and the regulatory attempt to remedy it. Thus, the ideal solution is therefore, whenever possible, to find a way of improving the functioning of markets without increasing the amount of regulation.

Potentially Competitive Markets. If it is competition, rather than ownership or legislation, that is the most important key to efficiency, then regulated activities can be reformed by opening them up to competition: existing regulation that suppresses competition can be removed, allowing competitive entry; existing corporate structures can be broken up into more competitive units; and new entrants can be encouraged into the markets of established regulated enterprises. However, this process is not straightforward; the problems of vertical linkages and incumbency are considerable.

Many monopolies exist not because they are, in the economic sense, "natural", but as a direct consequence of regulatory legislation prohibiting market entry. Regulatory protection may have been given to these activities because they were part of an organisation of which substantial parts were natural monopoly, or because the potentially competitive nature of the activity was not recognised. In such cases, the first step in restoring competition is to repeal the legislation protecting the monopoly.

In practice, however, the removal of legal obstacles to new competition alone has often not been sufficient to ensure real competition in former statutory monopolies. The incumbent may retain significant market power, arising, in particular, from technical, financial and brand-name advantages which may deter entry or make the experience of entrants unappealing.

Three issues may need to be tackled if competitive outcomes are to be achieved: the incumbent advantages described above; the use of revenues gained in non-competitive markets to cross-subsidize competitive activities; and the exploitation of vertical linkages to extend market power from areas which are natural monopolies to areas which are not (this might occur, for example, where one company owns both a transmission grid and the goods or services being transmitted). We examine each of these in turn.

The unexpected results of the deregulation of express coach services in the UK demonstrate clearly the extent of incumbent advantages. In this classically contestable industry, liberalisation failed to significantly reduce the market share of the major publicly owned carrier.[60] The incumbent, National Express strengthened its position by using the marketing advantages of its established national network, combined with exclusive or dominant access to city centre terminals. Together with an aggressive pricing policy, this enabled the company to resist new entrants. On routes where National Express — which

36

operated a universal brand name — had been the incumbent, successful entry was significantly lower than would have been expected given the industry's underlying cost structures. However, where the Scottish Bus Group, which used numerous local brand names, had been incumbent, successful entry was significantly greater and prices substantially lower than on routes where National Express was incumbent.[61]

This dominance has subsequently been tackled by a programme of fragmenting the business into regional operating companies. However, such a radical solution has been, to date, the exception rather than the rule — the breaking up of AT & T in the US and the privatisation and splitting-up of Japanese National Railways being the other notable examples.

The incumbent advantage resulting from the retention of a brand name adds a further complexity; one which is of greater importance than had been initially recognised. Following US airline deregulation, Levine[62] found that, despite higher unit costs than new entrants, the ten largest branded airlines after deregulation all "had brand names used by domestic airlines before deregulation, including those used by the four biggest carriers in the industry since 1934. The seven largest have the oldest brand (names)". With the demise of People Express, no new entrant generated more than 1 per cent of industry revenue. A major reason for the survival of these established carriers was the economics of information — people recognised a brandname they believed they could rely on. Indeed, Levine found that the confusion surrounding deregulation placed a premium on the ability to communicate efficiently through brand.

Combating this source of incumbent advantage presents new difficulties, however. Simply abolishing the brand name is unlikely to be an optimal solution. Brand names can benefit the consumer, as well as the supplier — recognition of a brandname reduces customer search costs. Thus, ending the use of the brand name will impose an additional cost on the consumer.

Cross-subsidisation is evident in electrical appliance retailing in the UK. Although its performance was often considerably poorer than that of its privately owned competitors, the public sector electricity industry has continued to occupy a major market position in retailing.[63] The financial strength stemming from its monopoly in the far larger market for electricity supply not only provides the industry with the resources to finance a continued presence in the appliance retailing market, but also weakens the constraint to improve performance which poor results might otherwise impose.

The problem of vertical linkages is illustrated powerfully by the failure to successfully liberalise the UK electricity industry in 1983. This failure stemmed from the interrelationship of transmission (natural monopoly) and generation (potentially competitive). To ensure access for competing suppliers on equal terms, the regulatory reform needed to recognise that both the national and domestic (local) distribution systems are natural monopolies. This it attempted to do, in the 1983 Energy Act, by allowing private generators of electricity to rent use of the public sector's distribution system on pre-specified terms, and by requiring the public sector electricity supply industry to purchase power from such independent producers on pre-specified terms related to its own avoidable costs of supply.

Although this attempt at liberalisation appeared to make electricity generation contestable, it did not make it so.[64] The public sector company's ownership of both the distribution networks and generating capacity led to the distortion of terms of competition in its favour: the terms of access to the transmission grids were set by the dominant incumbent in the generation business. As a result, only limited entry has taken place, generally in the form of small-scale by-product generation (e.g. using gas produced from refuse sites). However, it should be noted that new proposals have been put forward to restructure the generation and supply of electricity by separating generation from transmission, dividing existing generation between new companies and providing open access to transmission and distribution systems. These proposals have the aim of introducing competition into the industry as part of the privatisation of the industry under the Electricity Act 1989.

This suggests that competition policy must give a high priority to the separation of the ownership of genuine natural monopoly activities from those where competition is possible. This will foster the development of product market competition, for activities where this is technically feasible, and of effective capital market constraints on the company's performance. Furthermore, where the ownership of geographically distinct natural monopoly activities is separated, yardstick competition is possible from comparative information that is generated (for example, if each local electricity distribution network is separately owned, shareholders and regulators can evaluate the performance of their company in the light of the performance of a selection of comparable companies). However, the conditions under which yardstick competition is meaningful are strict, and practical opportunities may be limited.[65] Restructuring remains relatively underused in regulatory reform. Where it has been followed — for example, in the separation and privatisation of subsidiary road-haulage and ferry businesses from British Rail, and in the reconstruction of US telecommunications — it has usually been rewarded by improvements in the performance of the competitive activity.

Of course, even though a competitive outcome may be achievable, it may not be efficient. Establishing a market solution, perhaps modified by a relatively minor intervention may, nevertheless, be the appropriate policy. In particular, the licence under which a company trades may incorporate certain requirements to supply services that bring a public benefit, but no direct private benefit. The demand for universal service in some activities such as telephone services and gas supply is an obvious example.

In the debates on the privatisation of British Telecom, the issue of most apparent concern was the continued provision of public telephone service in rural areas. Provisions put into British Telecom's licence have inhibited the withdrawal of service, and in practice it also appears that British Telecom have regarded the supply of such services as useful in creating a public image as a company not concerned solely with profit.

Where the provision of basic utilities beyond the areas justified on strictly economic criteria is considered appropriate, therefore, this can be achieved by means far less extreme than nationalisation. Even where private firms fail to perceive public relations advantages or social obligations in such provision, other market-based solutions should provide the necessary impetus to tackle any limited non-commercial activities within a fundamentally commercial business. A good example is the supply of bus services to lightly trafficked areas, which is unprofitable but may be considered socially desirable. In several countries, specific subsidies are now given for the operation of such services on the basis of a competitive tender.

Natural Monopoly. In areas where competition is apparently impossible the competition authority is confronted with two questions. First, are existing competition rules effective in overseeing the industry? Second, if they are not, what regulatory structure is preferable, including public ownership? These are complex issues, as the current debate surrounding the privatisation of water in the UK demonstrates clearly. Some commentators argue that privatisation will bring clearer objectives and greater managerial autonomy. However, the regulatory framework that is envisaged is likely to be such that the regulator will, to a considerable extent, be active in the major decisions taken by the industry. Thus managerial autonomy may be severely compromised. A more effective solution may be public ownership combined with contracting out.

"Contracting out" (or franchising) is an attempt to introduce an element of competition to markets which are unavoidably monopolistic through setting up a competition for the market rather than competition in the market. The potential monopoly power and, hence, excess profits, of the successful firm are competed away in advance through the process of winning the contract. The competition authority is thus spared the regulatory pitfalls stemming from information asymmetry, as the bidding process forces the competing companies to reveal their true valuation of the contracted monopoly.

The advantages and disadvantages of contracting out have been widely discussed.[66] At its simplest, a contract or licence to undertake an activity is awarded, following an auction, to the bidder offering the largest monetary sum (although the authority offering the contract may also wish to take quality criteria into account). However, although this will transfer the monopoly profits that can be earned to the contracting authority, and allows price to be set by competition rather than regulatory decision, it does not remedy the distortions in market power and allocative efficiency associated with monopoly. The Chadwick-Demsetz franchise — in which the contract is awarded to the firm which offers to provide the service at the lowest consumer price (subject to quality considerations) — remedies this problem. The success of contracting out is dependent on a number of factors. First, there must be genuine competition for the contract. If there are insufficient competing firms, perhaps because of the specialised nature of the work, or if the incumbent firm is in a stronger position than its rivals (the incumbent's experience may enable it to operate at lower costs, or give its proposal greater credibility; it may also have better information than an outsider), then bidding may fail to reveal the true value of the contract. Even if there are sufficient firms of equal standing, however, competition may be undermined by collusion.[67]

Second, the contract must be clearly specified. Where this is not possible — technology may be changing rapidly, market demand may be fluctuating unpredictably, the contract may apply over an extended time-period — accountability and incentives may become blurred. This will necessitate some contractual flexibility, and continuing regulatory oversight is likely to be necessary.

Third, it must be possible to transfer a contract between firms cheaply and efficiently. Problems may arise where assets in which costs have been sunk have to be passed between companies on termination of a contract. The valuation of such assets is a complex and often expensive process, yet expectations about the accuracy of such valuation will have significant effects on the incumbent's incentives to invest, and on the decision of potential competitors to bid for the contract when it is reassessed. Anticipated over-valuation will lead the incumbent to over-invest, expected under-valuation will lead to under-investment, whilst uncertainty (greater riskiness) will also cause under-investment.

Some of these problems can be overcome by separating the ownership of sunk assets from the operations covered by the contract — which will become, in effect, an operating franchise. However, the separation of operating and sunk investment functions may not in practice be straightforward. Although the independent ownership of such assets enables effective contracting out of the operating franchise, it does not overcome the problems of market and regulatory failure associated with the provision of these assets.

Thus, contracting out is likely to be most appropriate when, first, the contracted-out activity is sufficiently similar to an existing private sector operation for tendering to generate effective competition in the provision of the requisite skills. Second, the competition authority must be able to define the activity to be provided with sufficient clarity for performance to be monitored effectively. However, in many areas where regulatory problems are greatest, franchising is also least effective: energy, telecommunications and water face a combination of technological and market change, and lengthy investment horizons. Nevertheless, in each of these industries there are activities that can be clearly specified, and closely parallel other non-regulated activities and should thus benefit from contracting out.

Contracting out therefore offers considerable potential in promoting competition in these activities, although this may most commonly be as part of a continuing regulatory framework. In many cases, including water supply and other utilities, the contracting out "option has often been rejected without due consideration despite its potential merits... (for) reasons... less to do with efficiency considerations than with other objectives of government and recalcitrant management".[68]

Where, for political or economic reasons, a government decides to retain an activity in the public sector, two further competition policy applications are relevant. Separate agencies should be set up, with distinct identities, to carry out these activities and a commercial culture should be encouraged wherever possible.

There are several reasons why this basic change in organisational structure might lead to improvements in performance. Agency-creation offers greater managerial independence, and reduces the degree of day-to-day political interference in decisions (although, clearly, the activity's inclusion in the public sector requires the government to retain ultimate responsibility). Dividing public sector activities into more coherent groupings enables greater operational flexibility — elements such as funding, salaries and career structures can be determined according to the needs of the particular agency rather than by universally applied public sector norms.

The process of establishing the agency also provides an important impetus for improved performance, as government is required to set clear organisational objectives for the agency management. This enables performance to be monitored from an economic perspective — noting costs, output etc. — and inefficient performance to be identified and remedied. This provides a sharp contrast to other government bodies in which objectives are often unclear, and the application of meaningful efficiency criteria thus rendered impractical.

Many of the benefits of regulatory reform have "come less from changes in structure or ownership as such than from changes in the culture with which these firms have operated". In the UK[69], changes in senior management led to the replacement of the established engineering-dominated culture with a commercial approach stressing marketing and finance. In industries ranging from steel via airways to postal services, overstaffing and bureaucracy have been sharply reduced as the organisations responded increasingly to market forces, both externally and internally. This suggests that competition authorities can generate considerable improvements in regulated companies, whether monopoly or not, by facilitating the impact of competitive market forces on management culture and organisational structure.

In summary, competition laws should be made to apply fully to sectors which are competitive or potentially competitive, once direct regulation has been abandoned. Competition policy should then take over the role of regulation to ensure that anti-competitive structures or behaviour do not emerge to inhibit the operation of market forces. Thus in sectors such as airlines, competition policy should focus on preventing mergers and acquisitions which restrict competition in particular markets, on doing away with commercial arrangements between airlines which restrict entry, capacity and fares as well as counteracting exclusionary behaviour such as denial of access to scarce airport or runway facilities or to computer reservation systems. In road transport, also, particular attention should be paid to the danger of predatory pricing on the part of dominant firms designed to keep out new entrants.

In sectors which display some natural monopoly features such as telecommunications, it is important after deregulation to ensure that predatory behaviour on the part of the incumbent monopoly does not inhibit new entry and that the profits from the still regulated segments of the industry are not used to subsidise competition in the deregulated parts (e.g. the equipment market or value added services). Special attention may also need to be given to vertical mergers in this industry to ensure that competition is not foreclosed in a particular market on account of the market power wielded by a dominant firm.

Section 7

Conclusions and Suggestions for Action

A number of important lessons can be learnt from the experience of regulatory reform within OECD Member countries. The purpose of deregulation and privatisation should be to pave the way for competition to emerge, and the most effective means of ensuring that it does so is to create market and industry structures that are competitive. Wherever possible, restructuring should precede deregulation or privatisation. Such restructuring can be desirable even where local or regional natural monopolies would remain by ensuring that the performance of the resulting firms in the industry can be compared.

A second lesson is that some activities of public or private monopolies may be made subject to competition, even if others are naturally monopolistic. Where competition is possible, the competitive activities should be separated from those of the monopoly. This division, which may be implemented by the creation of separate firms, will ensure that competition is not distorted by cross-subsidy from the monopolised sector and that no firm in the competitive sector is sheltered from the consequences of its own inefficiency. Competition laws should be fully applied to the competitive activities.

Competition authorities should be particularly vigilant in their implementation of merger policy. Merger activity is almost bound to be prominent in the period following deregulation. One positive reason for this may be the need for the deregulated firms to replace structures created by an environment of regulation with new organisations responding to market demands. In addition, the break-up of a firm prior to deregulation or privatisation may result in new firms which prove in practice to be in need of further restructuring for greater efficiency. Thus, desirable, efficiency-enhancing mergers may well arise following deregulation or privatisation. These mergers, however, like mergers in any sector, will need strict scrutiny by competition authorities to ensure that they are not anticompetitive.

One hoped-for result of deregulation in many sectors is the entry of new firms reducing concentration and stimulating competition. The newly competitive structure may be lost, however, if merger activity is not rigorously controlled. Anticompetitive mergers have in fact occurred in some markets following deregulation, especially where control over merger activity was not promptly transferred from the regulatory agency to the competition authorities.

The persistence of incumbent advantage after regulatory reform, which is proving to be substantial in a number of sectors, also places a strong responsibility on competition authorities to rigorously apply merger legislation; failure to do so may allow dominant firms in deregulated sectors to strengthen their positions through anticompetitive mergers.

Governments should be alert to the danger that incumbent advantage will be used to restrain competition. In many deregulated industries, previously regulated enterprises have continued to dominate by utilising predatory pricing and other forms of anticompetitive behaviour such as restricting access to important facilities. In such cases, additional pro-competitive regulatory reform may be necessary as well as effective competition legislation to deal with the conduct of dominant firms. Such cases call for the vigilant application of competition laws controlling monopolisation or abuse of a dominant position.

Predatory pricing merits particular attention. Normally, competition officials are and should be sceptical of allegations of predation, as most claims of predation turn out to involve desirable price competition and theory predicts that conditions allowing predation to succeed should be rare. Thus, the Committee on Competition Law and Policy recently recommended that allegations of predation be subjected to an analysis which would screen out most claims. That report also discussed, however, circumstances where predation might succeed, in particular where the dominant firm operates in multiple markets and where the new entrant has imperfect information about the dominant firm's costs. Where information is imperfect, predation may succeed because the new entrant will not know if the dominant firm is engaging in predatory tactics or is simply more efficient. Further, with multiple markets, the payoff to the dominant firm from establishing a reputation as a fearsome competitor is increased. What is important here is that these conditions which make successful predation somewhat more plausible may be more likely to be found in recently deregulated industries. This is especially true if the dominant firm controls scarce facilities such as terminals, reducing the likelihood of new entry in the post-predation period.

In addition, once government regulations are removed in a particular sector, competition policy enforcement should ensure that such regulations are not replaced by anticompetitive cartel-like agreements between firms to fix prices, restrict output or allocate markets. Firms which are used to cooperative arrangements under regulation (joint rate-fixing for example is often legal under regulation) may be expected to try to continue such cooperation, especially in the period immediately following deregulation. Competition authorities should pay particular attention to ensuring that such old habits are abandoned. The vigorous enforcement of prohibitions against cartel conduct is useful to this end.

Not all market failure may be overcome by structural reform or by reform of competition laws and the way they are enforced, however. Some regulatory intervention may remain essential to protect consumer welfare. However, such regulation that remains necessary should seek to encourage market forces wherever possible and not to restrict them.

Despite the attention regulatory reform has received during the past decade, many sectors in OECD Member countries remain relatively untouched by the reform movement. This can be seen in Part II of this report, which shows the extent of reforms undertaken since 1975 in the air and road transport, energy, posts and telecommunications sectors in 19 OECD Member countries and the EEC. From the information presented in Part II, it can be readily seen that extensive regulatory reforms in this sectors has been undertaken in only a handful of countries. The evidence summarised in this part of the report, however, shows that these reforms have been highly beneficial for efficiency and consumer welfare. Thus countries which have not yet engaged in widespread regulatory reform are urged strongly to do so.

Part II
Competition Policy and Deregulation

Regulatory Reform and Privatisation in OECD Countries

This part of the report has two functions. First, it provides details of recent regulatory reform and privatisation measures taken in OECD countries (over the period 1st October 1985 to end 1988). This serves to update the information contained in the Committee's 1986 report on Competition Policy and Deregulation. As in the latter report the information has been organised on a sector by sector basis, concentrating on five sectors which have been the object of a significant number of deregulatory initiatives — (1) energy, (2) transport (road, air and sea), (3) postal and telecommunications services, (4) banking and financial services and (5) radio and television broadcasting. Since three of these sectors — air and road transport and telecommunications — have been the object of individual study, the measures taken in these sectors have been dealt with very briefly, mainly giving more recent updating material since the air transport and telecommunications reports were published in 1988. The reader is referred to the three reports for more details of the regulatory reforms undertaken in each country in these sectors. In addition, a comprehensive account of reforms in OECD countries in the banking sector is contained in a recent OECD study[70].

The measures that are included here concern:

i)   Proposed or actual legislation on the partial or total reform of regulations relating to control of entry, price or output in the above-mentioned sectors;

ii)   The privatisation of enterprises;

iii)   The extension of competition laws to deal with restrictive behaviour in these sectors as well as actual cases of enforcement (this also includes interventions by competition authorities before regulatory boards or commissions).

The countries contributing to this survey were Australia, Austria, Belgium, Canada, Denmark, Finland, France, Germany, Ireland, Japan, New Zealand, Norway, Portugal, Spain, Sweden, Switzerland, Turkey, the United Kingdom, the United States and the EEC.

The second function of this part is to provide a picture of how far governments have gone in regulatory reform since the reform movement began in earnest in the 1970s. Seventeen tables give a graphic representation of the extent of regulation and public ownership in the transport (airlines, buses and road freight), posts and telecommunications and energy sectors. For comparison, the situation in 1975 is presented alongside the current (1990) position. The countries included in these charts are the same as those mentioned in the preceding paragraph except for France, Portugal and Spain and with the addition of Turkey.

In interpreting the tables, it should be noted that they are limited to domestic markets; international markets are excluded. Also, countries with federal systems were asked to report on regulation only at the federal level. The situation at the provincial, State or local

47

level is described in the text but the tables themselves reflect only the situation at national level. This is particularly significant in transport and energy generation, transmission and distribution which are frequently regulated at the provincial or local level.

For other matters relevant to the interpretation of the tables the reader is referred to the Appendix, which presents the definitions which countries were asked to follow when supplying information.

48

Energy

Australia

Note that in Table 1 the transport of refined petroleum in some States is undertaken to a large extent by the State rail systems which are State government owned monopolies (in four of the six States — in the other two States the Federally owned railway operates in competition with other modes), but some transportation is by privately owned road haulage or a mix of modes (e.g. rail transport to terminals from whence it is distributed by road). As regards the gas industry (see Table 2), the production and distribution is unregulated in all States in 1990 except for prices of transmission in South Australia. The prices for the distribution of gas are partially regulated in four States and unregulated in two others while entry is regulated in four States and unregulated in two others, these being Queensland and Tasmania.

Austria

In electricity generation (Table 3 below), maximum prices only are set by the regulatory authorities, but lower prices are permitted. As regards entry to the industry, in principle this is free but in act new licences to applicants are awarded only for areas for which a licence has not

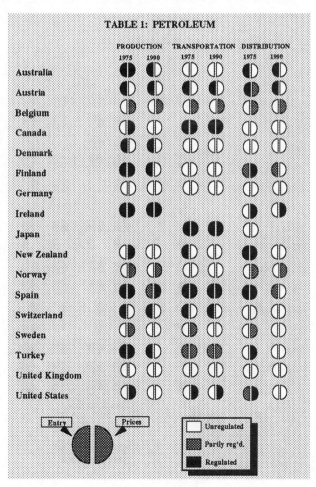

TABLE 1: PETROLEUM

already been given because each regional utility has a monopoly under the present structure of the Austrian electricity industry. Enterprises which wish to generate electricity for their own consumption however do not require a licence. Any surplus electricity may be sold to the public electricity supplier but may not be sold directly to consumers without the authorisation of the public supplier.

Canada

Following the 1 June 1985 deregulation of oil prices and the lifting of controls on short-term oil exports, Canadian natural gas markets were deregulated on 1 October 1986. Since then, prices for sales to both domestic and export markets have been determined by direct buyer-seller negotiations. In September 1987, the National Energy Board (NEB) adopted a market-based procedure that highlights the role of market forces in determination of both the terms and levels of gas exports.

Since the commencement of these deregulatory efforts, toll and tariff issues have been totally deregulated for 32 of the 42 pipelines under NEB jurisdiction. These pipelines are now regulated on a complaints basis only.

Following the 31 October 1985 Agreement on Natural Gas Markets and Prices between the federal and provincial governments leading to the deregulation of field prices of natural gas, a Pipeline Review Panel was established to review the role of interprovincial and international pipelines engaged in the buying, selling, and transportation of gas. The Panel's report presented in June 1986, recommended the separation of a pipeline's marketing function from its transportation function, and that a pipeline's marketing arm should contract with its transportation arm for transportation services. This separation of functions in the Canadian gas market is a fundamental and important change of focus for both federal and provincial regulatory boards, following increased levels of

TABLE 2: GAS

	PRODUCTION 1975	PRODUCTION 1990	TRANSPORTATION 1975	TRANSPORTATION 1990	DISTRIBUTION 1975	DISTRIBUTION 1990
Austria						
Belgium						
Canada						
Denmark						
Finland						
Germany						
Ireland						
Japan						
New Zealand						
Spain						
Switzerland						
Sweden						
Turkey						
United Kingdom						
United States						

Entry — Prices

Legend:
- Unregulated
- Partly reg'd.
- Regulated

50

competition in gas markets. Recognising the importance of the federally elucidated principle with respect to the matters within its jurisdiction, the Ontario Energy Board in March 1989 ordered local gas distributors to separate their transportation and marketing functions for future hearings.

In addition to the important recommendations on structural separation, the June 1986 Report of the Pipeline Review Panel recommended non-discriminatory access to pipeline transportation, and the "unbundling" of transportation services.

The current situation in Canada (see Tables 1 and 2) is that entry to petroleum and gas pipeline transport is regulated in relation to expansion of pipelines and partly regulated as regards source of transportation. Moreover, prices and entry conditions relating to the distribution of gas and the generation, transmission and distribution of electricity are regulated at the provincial level, the Federal government having jurisdiction only over interprovincial shipments and transport. Provincial state monopolies exist in the electricity sector.

Finland

The Ministry of Trade and Industry has set up a permanent working party dealing with energy issues to cooperate with the Office of Free Competition.

Price control of oil products was abolished 1st October 1988. At present, both Neste, the state-owned oil refining company, and the oil distribution companies are in a position to decide on their prices independently.

The prices of heating oil and heavy fuel oil were previously equalised by an equalisation fund. This procedure was abolished as of 31 December 1988.

The producers of electricity agreed in January 1989 on the new slightly more liberal conditions of transmission of electricity by the power-distribution network. The conditions have been published as recommendations.

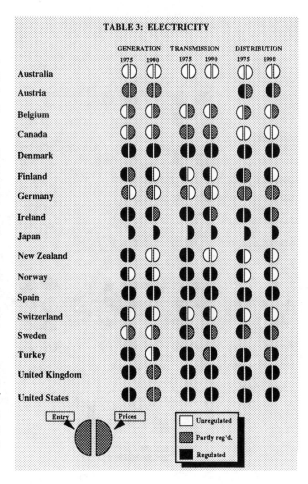

51

France

Until recently the distribution of oil was highly regulated in France by an Act of 1928 which gave a monopoly to the State in the importation of oil. This monopoly was delegated essentially to the major oil companies but also some independents were authorised under strict conditions. Detailed requirements were prescribed for the refining, supply stocking and transport of oil and retail prices of petrol were strictly controlled until 1985.

1976 saw the first moves to deregulate oil distribution when the main general retail distributors were authorised to import refined oil products. All the major retail chains established subsidiaries in order to purchase petrol abroad or at home and this became a significant competitive factor. At the end of 1988, they had acquired 35 per cent of the retail market. In 1976, the price of heavy fuel oil was decontrolled.

In 1985, the most significant deregulation occurred when all petrol prices were freed. This measure was the direct result of the competition that had emerged from the supermarkets.

In 1986, the regulations requiring 90 per cent of petroleum to be refined on national territory and independent importers to obtain 80 per cent of their supplies from refineries established in the EEC were abolished.

In 1987, liberalisation of the conditions for the importation of petroleum products by independents: extension of the term of validity of the licence from three to five years and simplified procedure for the obtaining of a licence.

In 1988, advertising of petrol was allowed.

There was also a reform of safety stocks requirement. Importers and refiners are still subject to the requirement that they must hold 90 days' stock of supplies but a common organisation was established to look after 45 days' stocks. Thus the risk of a fall in prices is partly shared by all.

TABLE 4: PETROL OWNERSHIP

	PRODUCTION		TRANSPORTATION		DISTRIBUTION	
	1975	1990	1975	1990	1975	1990
Australia	Private	Private	Private	Private	Private	Private
Austria	Mixed	Mixed	Mixed	Mixed	Mixed	Mixed
Canada	Private	Mixed	Private	Private	Private	Mixed
Denmark	Private	Private	Private	Private	Private	Private
Finland	Public	Public	Mixed	Mixed	Private	Mixed
Germany	Private	Private	Private	Private	Private	Private
Ireland	Public	Public	Private	Private	Private	Private
Japan	Private	Private	Private	Private	Private	Private
New Zealand	Private	Private	Private	Private	Private	Private
Norway	Private	Mixed	Private	Mixed	Private	Mixed
Spain	Mixed	Mixed	Public	Mixed	Public	Mixed
Switzerland	Mixed	Mixed	Mixed	Mixed	Private	Private
Sweden	Mixed	Mixed	Mixed	Mixed	Mixed	Mixed
Turkey	Mixed	Mixed	Mixed	Mixed	Mixed	Mixed
United Kingdom	Mixed	Private	Private	Private	Private	Private
United States	Private	Private	Private	Private	Private	Private

Legend:
□ Privately owned
▨ Mixed
■ Publicly owned

Germany

In Germany, under the 1980 amendment to the Act against Restraints of Competition, electricity, gas, and water supply agreements, exempt from the general ban on cartel agreements, were made subject to time limits; new agreements must be notified to the cartel authorities, which may then prohibit all or part of them if they contain anticompetitive elements. The agreements for allocating supply areas are now limited to 20-year terms, after which they must be rereported to the cartel authorities; the latter may void them if it considers them to be detrimental to competition.

In the fifth law to amend the Cartel Act, provisions have been laid down for further strengthening competition among energy suppliers. Whenever the concessions granted to any given utility by local authorities expire, a change to another utility is now facilitated. This should ensure genuine competition on supply markets.

The alteration of the federal rates' schedule for the electricity sector aims at making the base rate no longer dependent on elements largely independent of consumption (such as the number of rooms in houses, the connected load in business, area under cultivation in agriculture), but on the electricity actually used. The change eliminates the control checks used to determine the previously decisive elements and contributes to ensuring the economical use of energy by households and small business. Prices are regulated as regards household consumption and entry to the industry requires a government licence under the energy legislation in force.

There exists a wide variety of forms of ownership in the electricity sector, including purely private companies, municipally owned and state owned companies. There have been several privatisations in the energy sector in recent years, notably the complete privatisation of VIAG and VEBA. The Government no longer has any significant holdings in the electricity and gas sectors, although some Laender governments and local authorities have stakes in supply companies. In the oil sector, the

TABLE 5: GAS OWNERSHIP

	PRODUCTION 1975	PRODUCTION 1990	TRANSPORTATION 1975	TRANSPORTATION 1990	DISTRIBUTION 1975	DISTRIBUTION 1990
Australia	Privately	Privately				
Austria	Mixed	Mixed	Mixed	Mixed	Mixed	Mixed
Canada	Privately	Privately	Privately	Privately	Privately	Privately
Denmark	Publicly	Publicly	Publicly	Publicly	Publicly	Publicly
Finland	Publicly	Publicly	Publicly	Publicly	Publicly	Publicly
Germany	Privately	Privately	Privately	Privately	Privately	Privately
Ireland		Publicly		Publicly		Publicly
Japan	Privately	Privately	Privately	Privately	Privately	Privately
New Zealand	Mixed	Mixed	Publicly	Privately	Mixed	Mixed
Spain	Publicly	Publicly	Publicly	Publicly	Publicly	Publicly
Switzerland	Mixed	Mixed	Mixed	Mixed	Mixed	Mixed
Sweden	Privately	Privately		Publicly	Privately	Privately
Turkey		Publicly	Publicly	Publicly	Publicly	Publicly
United Kingdom	Mixed	Privately	Publicly	Privately	Publicly	Privately
United States	Privately	Privately	Privately	Privately	Privately	Privately

Legend:
☐ Privately owned
▦ Mixed
■ Publicly owned

53

Federal government has no stake in oil companies, while it continues to have a 75 per cent interest in one coal producer — Saarbergwerk AG.

New Zealand

Electricity

In 1987 the government created the state-owned Electricity Corporation ("Electricorp") to take over the ownership and operation of the electricity generation and transmission activities of the Ministry of Energy. In addition legal impediments to entry into generation markets were removed.

While the government-owned corporation controls 94 per cent of New Zealand's generating capacity, any other business is forced to build its own generating facility though none have yet done so. The transmission sector as of 1st January 1990 was also completely owned by Electricorp. The distribution sector is predominantly owned by local government bodies, though there are plans to privatise these.

In 1989 the government announced further changes. First the ownership of the grid is to be separated from Electricorp's generating business. The grid will be owned by a club of generators with each owning up to a third of the capital. The remainder will be open to other investors. Secondly the area franchise system, which grants statutory monopolies to local bodies, will be dismantled. Thirdly distributors will be required to introduce two-part tariffs comprising an energy charge and a line charge.

Natural gas

In 1989 the government announced three major changes. First, the area franchise system is to be removed. Secondly, government control over the construction of pipelines is to be removed. Thirdly, government control over the use of pipelines by third parties is to be abolished.

TABLE 6: ELECTRICITY OWNERSHIP

	GENERATION 1975	GENERATION 1990	TRANSMISSION 1975	TRANSMISSION 1990	DISTRIBUTION 1975	DISTRIBUTION 1990
Australia	Publicly	Publicly	Publicly	Publicly	Publicly	Publicly
Austria	Publicly	Publicly	Publicly	Publicly	Publicly	Publicly
Canada	Publicly	Publicly	Publicly	Publicly	Publicly	Publicly
Denmark	Publicly	Publicly	Publicly	Publicly	Publicly	Publicly
Finland	Mixed	Mixed	Publicly	Mixed	Privately	Privately
Germany	Mixed	Mixed	Publicly	Publicly	Mixed	Mixed
Ireland	Publicly	Publicly	Publicly	Publicly	Publicly	Publicly
Japan	Privately	Privately	Privately	Privately	Privately	Privately
New Zealand	Mixed	Publicly	Publicly	Publicly	Publicly	Publicly
Norway	Mixed	Mixed	Publicly	Publicly	Publicly	Publicly
Spain	Mixed	Mixed	Publicly	Publicly	Mixed	Mixed
Switzerland	Mixed	Mixed	Mixed	Mixed	Mixed	Mixed
Sweden	Mixed	Mixed	Publicly	Publicly	Mixed	Mixed
Turkey	Mixed	Publicly	Mixed	Mixed	Mixed	Publicly
United Kingdom	Publicly	Publicly	Publicly	Publicly	Publicly	Publicly
United States	Mixed	Mixed	Mixed	Mixed	Mixed	Mixed

Privately owned
Mixed
Publicly owned

Common carrier issues will be left to general competition law, which is likely to lead to the application of principles established under the American essential facilities doctrine.

Portugal

Since 1988 it has been possible for private individuals or for public or private enterprises, in addition to the public enterprise EDP, to engage in the production of electricity, provided that the plant used to generate the electricity does not exceed 10 000 kw installed power. Since end 1988 a more flexible pricing system has been introduced into the electricity industry.

Spain

Petroleum

Since 1986, the import of petroleum products, which was formerly reserved for the State monopoly CAMPSA, has been liberalised to allow new entrants subject to authorisation. Until the transitional period agreed with the EEC ends, authorised foreign operators are limited by progressive import quotas which restrict competition with domestic producers.

After the reorganisation of the monopoly prior to entry into the EEC, the pipeline network became the property of CAMPSA. Afterwards, as a result of the liberalizing commitments undertaken at the time of entry and after a series of disputes with the Directorate General of Competition of the EC, the use of pipelines by authorised private operators (domestic or foreign) was permitted, although the ownership of the network is still in the hands of CAMPSA.

The price of oil products was among those subject to government control. This situation will change soon as liberalization is planned for June 1990, although the government will continue fixing a ceiling guide price.

In 1988, two pieces of legislation (Royal Decree 645/88 and Royal Decree-Law 4/88) were designed to regulate wholesale and retail trade in petroleum products following the relaxing of the State petroleum monopoly CAMPSA. The legislation was designed to ensure that private distributors would have an adequate national coverage for their operations on a non-discriminatory basis compared with retail outlets owned or operated by CAMPSA.

Natural gas

The recent Law on gaseous hydrocarbons establishes the activities of production, piping and distribution of natural gas as a public service. In some cases, and subject to obtaining the appropriate administrative concession, the carrying out of these activities may be entrusted to public or private bodies.

The selling price to the public of natural gas is set according to a formula which takes into account the current prices of gas oil and fuel oil. This is intended to encourage the use of natural gas as a power source, particularly by large consumers, by means of a competitive price. In addition, the price of butane gas, used in many homes and supplied in containers, was liberalized from 1 January 1990.

United Kingdom

Gas

In 1986, British Gas Corporation was privatised and a new regulatory authority, the Office of Gas Supply (OFGAS) established to oversee the industry. The Gas Act 1986 lays down a system for authorising the supply of gas subject to regulatory conditions. The conditions distinguish between the tariff (consumption up to 25,000 therms per annum) and contract (consumption of more than 25,000 therms) sectors of the gas supply market. The tariff sector was made subject to a system of price control in view of the limited scope for competition associated with supply to consumers who take small quantities of gas. In the contract sector British Gas was required to publish certain information on pricing but was otherwise free to negotiate contracts with customers. At the same time, the contract sector was subject to the provisions of the competition legislation.

In November 1987, the Director General of Fair Trading made a reference of the supply of gas to non-tariff customers (primarily large industrial users) to the Monopolies and Mergers Commission under the monopoly provisions of the Fair Trading Act 1973. The Commission's report was published in October 1988. It found that British Gas had practised extensive discrimination in the pricing and supply of gas to non-tariff customers, and that this was against the public interest. The main recommendations of the MMC were that British Gas should be required:

— To publish a price schedule at which it is prepared to supply firm and interruptible gas to contract customers, and not to discriminate in pricing or supply;

— Not to refuse to supply interruptible gas on the basis of the use made of the gas, or the alternative fuel available;

— To publish further information on common carriage terms;

— To contract initially for no more than 90 per cent of any new gas fields.

The changes recommended by the report were implemented in early 1989 following discussions between British Gas and the Director General of Gas Supply. The recommendation that British Gas should not contract initially for more than 90 per cent of any new gas fields was implemented in a modified form. The Government has set as a target that 10 per cent of all new gas (contracted from 1 June 1989) should be supplied to the market by suppliers other than British Gas. The target covers gas both from the UK continental shelf and imported, and includes gas carried both by British Gas on a common carrier basis, and by any new dedicated pipelines that may be built by carriers other than British Gas. The position will be reviewed after a two-year period.

Electricity

Since the adoption of the Electricity Act in July 1989, the UK electricity industry is in the process of being returned to the private sector, under a regime which will allow full competition in both generation and supply. In particular it is of note that:

Generation. The existing generating company, the Central Electricity Generating Board, will be divided into four separate licensed companies. Three of these will be generating companies. In addition others will be able to hold licences and to operate as generators, so that competition in generation will be fulfilled. Prices for generation will not be regulated but the Director General of Electricity Supply will be responsible for promotion of competition between generators. Small generators and de-minimis suppliers, who do not have a significant impact on the system, and own generators will be exempt from the requirement to hold a licence.

Transmission. The fourth company created from the CEGB will be a separate transmission company owned by the public electricity supply companies (see distribution below) but independently operated. Transmission prices will be subject to an "RPI-X" formula.

Distribution. The assets of the existing Area Electricity Boards, responsible for the retail distribution of electricity to producers, will be vested in licensed public electricity supply companies with similar geographic locations. Their prices will be subject to an "RPI-X" formula. Others will also be able to obtain licences to supply electricity to premises.

Electricity prices are not set by the government at this time but financial targets are agreed for the industry, which determines its own prices to meet these targets. There has been some provision for entry into the market of some private generators since 1983. All generating companies, the transmission company and the public electricity supply companies will be privately owned after flotation with the exception of the generating company controlling the industry's nuclear capacity, which will remain in public ownership.

United States

Both the Antitrust Division and the Federal Trade Commission have been active in intervening in proceedings involving the oil and gas industries before the Federal Energy Regulatory Commission (FERC) as well as issuing reports and proposals aimed at deregulating activities in these industries.

In 1987, the Division filed comments supporting a proposal by FERC to permit regulated producers and purchasers of natural gas to discontinue, upon 30 days' written notice after the expiration of their contractual obligations, the sale or purchase of natural gas. Under existing regulations the parties to a natural gas supply contract must continue to observe its provisions after the contract expires until FERC explicitly permits the parties to abandon their obligations. The Division argued that the proposed rule change was consistent with the competitive nature of the natural gas production market and would enhance the ability of the market to allocate efficiently natural gas supplies. FERC issued final orders adopting its proposals on 5 February 1988 and 22 July 1988.

The Federal Trade Commission's staff advised FERC that market rivals may be able to use the agency's regulatory process to impede competition in the distribution of natural gas. In one example, the staff cited a case where two pipeline operators petitioned FERC to block entry of a third pipeline into their marketing area. The staff suggested that by involving a rival in prolonged, expensive, and possibly meritless legal action, existing competitors might successfully deter entry into a market and reduce competition.

During 1989, the Division continued to participate in proceedings before FERC concerning the construction of new natural gas pipeline capacity to California. New regulations were established by the FERC to expedite new pipeline service. The Department of Justice supported new applications filed under these regulations, arguing that the public interest and the interest of direct and indirect consumers of natural gas would be best served if the FERC gave permission to each of three competing applicants to build a new interstate pipeline to California. The Department argued that the market would determine how increased natural gas demand in California would be most efficiently served. The Department also asked the Commission to permit the applicants to operate under contracts negotiated with the proposed customers without regulatory intervention by the Commission. In January 1990, the FERC approved all of the outstanding applications.

In January 1989, the Division intervened in two proceedings initiated by applicants seeking to build new natural gas pipelines from Canada to the Northeast United States and to New England. The Division asked the FERC to consider whether partial ownership of the new lines by potentially competing pipelines originating in the Gulf Coast could lessen competition in Northeast and New England natural gas markets. As of January 1990, the Commission had yet to order hearings on the applications.

The Division also filed comments on a FERC proposal concerning the brokering of interstate natural gas pipeline capacity. In recent years, gas transportation (as opposed to gas sales) has become an important part of the interstate pipeline business. The FERC proposal would allow certain holders of transportation rights on interstate gas pipelines to resell those rights. The Division's comments supported this proposal, pointing out that brokering will benefit society by increasing competition in the sale of gas transportation and by making more efficient the allocation of gas pipeline capacity. The Division also urged FERC to adopt rules that would reduce the likelihood that firms could exercise market power in brokering transactions, and argued that FERC should not impose price caps on such brokering until experience had shown whether such regulation was necessary. The Federal Trade Commission also supported the FERC proposal, telling FERC that permitting the sales of the rights would reallocate them to those who value them the most, and would likely expand the array of available gas transportation services in a way that would result in more efficient markets. As of the end of 1989, FERC had taken no action.

In May 1989, the Division intervened in the proposed merger of Southern California Edison Company and San Diego Gas and Electric Company. The proposed combination would form the largest privately owned electric utility in the United States. The Division has yet to take a position on the proposed merger, but has focused on whether the transaction would allow the merged company to better evade regulation and whether the merger would reduce competition in the sale and transmission of bulk power. A hearing was scheduled to begin in February 1990.

Transport

A. Road

Australia

In Australia the Federal Government has no direct involvement in economic regulation of land transport modes — rail, road, passenger buses and trucking. Federal Government regulation is only concerned with safety matters. The inter-State Commission completed an investigation into road vehicle regulations in June 1988. The Federal Government's response to the findings of the Commission included establishing nationally uniform technical and operational regulations for the first time.

However, State and local government bodies in Australia have regulated entry and services of passenger buses on local, metropolitan and intercity routes, varying in extent from State to State. In some States also heavy road freight transport is subject to regional permits and/or some major items of freight, such as grain and coal, have been reserved to the publicly owned rail system of the State concerned. In general, recent trends have been toward reduced economic regulation at State and local government level.

Inter-city bus services are mainly performed by privately owned operators. Local bus services are provided by State Government owned authorities and private operators to an extent varying from State to State.

Austria

As regards inter-city and local buses, the regulatory authorities routinely approve fares, routes and capacity that are notified, while entry to the sectors is subject only to a fit, willing and able requirement.

Canada

On 1 January 1988, the NTA and the MVTA went into effect. These new Acts were designed to encourage economic growth and development in transportation by placing a greater reliance on competition.

In particular, the NTA allowed for the replacement of collective rate-making in railways by the use of confidential contracts, and for an improvement in shipper remedies.

59

In trucking, the MVTA aims at the exclusive use of "fitness" criteria in extra-provincial truck licensing by 1992, the elimination of rate control for extra-provincial trucking, and the removal of obligations to approve or publish extra-provincial trucking rates. Although the MVTA is in effect federally, provincial governments are still at the initial stages of implementing the Act within their own jurisdiction. Other trucking initiatives included efforts in October 1987 and February 1988 to standardise Canadian motor carrier safety rules, and the sizes of trucks operated in Canada.

Inter-city buses and local buses are regulated at the provincial and municipal levels respectively.

Denmark

Road freight transport was substantially deregulated as from 1st January 1989, when the former rules on control of entry conditions, capacity, rates and prices were repealed. Since that date, the Monopolies and Restrictive Practices Supervision Act applies fully to the road freight transport sector.

Finland

In the period 1 October 1985 to 31 December 1988, there have been some deregulatory actions in the road traffic sector. The regulation of road freight has traditionally been comprehensive and dates from 1919. The basic conditions for awarding licences are that there is a public need for an additional service as well as the fitness and competence assessment of the applicant. In examining the need for a new entrant the trade association in question is asked for its views. As a result entry into the industry is almost impossible except through acquisition. The rates are fixed by the authorities for specialised services and for consignments weighing less than five tons in scheduled traffic.

At the beginning of 1988, the award of freight traffic licences was liberalised to allow carriers to transport freight without geographical restrictions and to extend the traffic rights granted to carriers operating scheduled services.

In 1988, the Ministry of Transport and Communications began a review of the public need requirement for awarding road freight licences.

France

There have been two significant reforms in the freight sector :
— Abolition of the mandatory tariff system as from 1 January 1989,
— Abolition of the quota system for licensing long distance services.

Ireland

The 1986 Road Transport Act has liberalised the licensing of the merchandise road haulage business. The Carrier's licence is freely available to all applicants who satisfy the

EC requirements of professional competence, good repute and appropriate financial standing. It is unrestricted as to the number of vehicles operated, the type of merchandise carried and the area of operation.

As regards inter-city and local bus services, fares are partly regulated in the sense that there is commercial freedom to set fares provided they do not exceed certain maximum approved limits. As regards routes and scheduling, there is no capacity limit for approved routes. In relation to buses, the State-owned company (CIE) is free of restrictions and licensing requirements except that it may not initiate or alter a service to compete directly with a licensed private operator. CIE fares are subject to maximum approved limits. The relevant legislation on access to the market for bus services, both inter-city and local, is being reviewed.

Japan

In 1989, two bills aimed at deregulating motor freight transport and freight forwarding were passed by the Diet. The present regulations governing entry to trucking will be relaxed. The provision on supply and demand balance will be lifted and the certificate system will be changed to a permission system. In the case of smaller carriers, a notification system will be adopted. Concerning rates and prices, the present authorisation system will be changed to a prenotification system. Similar reforms are proposed for the freight forwarding sector. As regards the application of the Anti-Monopoly Act, the business of freight forwarding will not be exempted in the new law.

With regard to railways, the Japanese National Railways has been split up into six passenger railways companies and one freight company which have been privatised.

TABLE 7: TRANSPORT I

	INTER-CITY BUSES		LOCAL BUSES	
	1975	1990	1975	1990
Australia				
Austria				
Canada				
Denmark				
Finland				
Germany				
Ireland				
Japan				
New Zealand				
Norway				
Spain				
Switzerland				
Sweden				
Turkey				
United Kingdom				
United States				

Legend: Entry / Service / Prices (pie segments)

Unregulated
Partly reg'd.
Regulated

61

New Zealand

Taxi services

Price control and quantitative licensing of taxi services were abolished under the Transport Services Licensing Act 1989 and have been replaced with a licensing system using public safety and service criteria. New entrants no longer need to buy a licence from an existing operator.

Bus services

The Local Government Amendment (No 4) Act 1989 requires local authorities to separate out their commercial passenger transport businesses as separate companies by mid-1991. Regional councils will not be able to have any interest in any passenger transport operations.

Norway

Goods traffic

On 1 January 1987, the system of licensing trucks and ships for the transport of goods was liberalised. The notion of routes was abandoned as was also the special permit for undertaking scheduled transport of goods by truck. As a consequence the approval of tariffs in such transport ceased to apply. Permission to run a transport business is now given on objective criteria and is no longer limited to a particular region. The system of permits for acting as intermediaries between transporter and carrier, for groupage traffic (haulage) and for freight by ship has been completely removed.

For scheduled passenger transport a licence is still necessary. The definition of such transport was changed on 1 January 1987 introducing the criterion of openness, meaning that a licence is required to operate a transport service which is open to the public as a scheduled transport service.

A licence is also necessary for taxis, limousine services and transport of disabled persons.

The legal authority to oblige firms running coaches for hire to join a central organisation has been removed. The Ministry of Transport and Communication has also recommended that geographical boundaries be removed.

The system of permits for transport service by hotels, ambulance service and car hire no longer applies.

The Ministry of Transport and Communication has recommended the forming of a committee to evaluate the use of tendering in scheduled transport.

Portugal

The most significant deregulatory change in the transport of goods by railways, road and combined road/rail and inland waterway occurred on 17 December 1986 with the coming into force of Decree/Law No. 415-A which allowed carriers freedom to set their own prices.

For passenger transport, whether by bus, tram, trolleybus, underground train or taxi, fares are fixed by the competent national authorities. Similar local public transport fares are fixed by the local authorities.

In addition, the Portuguese Parliament is discussing a fundamental reform of road transport which would repeal a 1945 Act regulating conditions of entry to the road transport sector.

Spain

In 1975, and in general before the adoption of the Law regulating Land Transport of 1987, the Government fixed compulsory tariffs for application on regular passenger transport services. There were maximum tariffs for non-regular passenger transport (discretionary transport). The new law provides that the government may establish compulsory or reference tariffs which can consist of single or maximum and/or minimum amounts when reasons relating to the organisation of transport make it advisable. When these tariffs do not exist, the market price will be applied. Moreover, a wide-reaching mechanism has been established for tariff reviews which can be put into effect officially or on application from interested parties whether individual or general.

The previous system required the granting of a licence to be able to operate as a carrier. Although the licensing system was fairly rigid and restrictive, in practice it was not applied in this manner and licences were granted almost automatically, which has had a great influence in the atomization of the industry. At present a licence is still required,

TABLE 8: TRANSPORT II

	TRUCKING		AIRLINES	
	1975	1990	1975	1990
Australia				
Austria				
Canada				
Denmark				
Finland				
Germany				
Ireland				
Japan				
New Zealand				
Norway				
Spain				
Switzerland				
Sweden				
Turkey				
United Kingdom				
United States				

Entry — Service — Prices

Unregulated
Partly reg'd.
Regulated

63

although access is unrestricted, and only the following conditions need be fulfilled by the licensee:

— Spanish national, or national of other country in the case of which, under international treaties or agreements signed by Spain, this condition is not required.
— Professional training, honesty and economic means.
— Comply with the tax, labour and social obligations required by the legislation in force.
— Those specifically relating to transport.

However, at certain times and when certain specific circumstances in the Law occur, the Government may restrict or make access to transport conditional, generally or in relation to particular types of activities and services. The circumstances above-mentioned are as follows:

— Imbalances between demand and supply which prevent the correct provision of service.
— When an increase in supply may originate imbalances and failures.
— When adequate operation of the transport system requires an appropriate size of firms.
— For reasons of economic policy.
— When the operation of the transport system as a whole may be harmed.

Regular passenger transport services were and are subject to administrative concessions for a limited period. The concession specifies the frequency and the stops. However, non-regular transport (discretionary) is subject to authorisation under a much more liberal scheme.

The management and arrangement of urban and inter-urban passenger transport is in the hands of local authorities. The operation is carried out almost always in the form of a monopoly either directly by the local authority itself or by arrangement with a mixed public/private undertaking. Legislation in force has abolished the restrictions on routes, truck loads, etc.

In 1975, the railway companies Renfe and Feve, under their preferential right of purchase legally recognised for the railways in a clear attempt to promote railway services, were owners of a large network of bus routes and the corresponding fleets of buses. In 1990 the real situation has not changed, although by the Law regulating Land Transport, ENATCAR (Empresa Nacional de Transporte de Viajeros por Carretera) was created and took over the concessions and fleets held up to then by Renfe and Feve. Like its predecessors, ENATCAR competes with the private concessionary carriers.

Compared with 1975, the public/private ownership situation in air transport has changed significantly. In that year, the State-owned companies Iberia and Aviaco had only one competitor — the private charter carrier Spantax. In the last decade, backed by the tourist boom, a number of private charter carriers have come into being which, together, now absorb an important and growing part of the traffic — normally international — of passengers and goods.

Sweden

The road freight transport industry has been deregulated step by step during the last decades. Regulatory control over maximum rates was abolished in 1972 and entry has been liberalised gradually since the 1960s. In 1987, the last remaining process concerning the public need test before entry was abolished. It concerned mainly freight forwarders (agencies). Still there is a process called "fitness" testing to go through before entry.

Within the sector of taxi services a decision was taken in 1988 to implement deregulation measures beginning on 1 July 1990. Rates regulation and entry control based on testing of the public need will then be abolished. The remaining control will be a fitness testing of applicants for a licence.

Also regulation of bus and coach traffic has been further liberalised during the last few years. For scheduled local bus services, the monopoly licence system expired in 1989 and was replaced by a tendering system in most areas. The service conditions and fares are usually fixed in the invitations to tender. Tenderers thus compete on the price they require for the service during a given period, i.e. the amount of public subsidy required. Scheduled inter-city coach services, though, are only allowed if they do not harm established railway traffic or mass-transport services operated by county traffic organisations. If the county traffic organisation operates bus services itself, no licence is needed but on the other hand there is no competition in these cases. Chartered bus traffic is not regulated.

United Kingdom

The 1985 Transport Act totally deregulated local buses outside London by abolishing the road service licensing system and replacing it by a system of registration of local bus services without a right of objection. The Act also changed the basis for according subsidies for unprofitable services by putting them out to competitive tender. London buses are planned for deregulation in the early 1990s and the

TABLE 9: TRANSPORT OWNERSHIP

	INTER CITY BUSES		LOCAL BUSES		TRUCKING		AIRLINES	
	1975	1990	1975	1990	1975	1990	1975	1990
Australia	Private	Private	Private	Private	Private	Private	Mixed	Mixed
Austria	Mixed	Mixed	Mixed	Mixed	Private	Private	Public	Mixed
Canada	Private	Private	Private	Private	Private	Private	Public	Private
Denmark	Public	Public	Mixed	Mixed	Private	Private	Mixed	Mixed
Finland	Mixed	Mixed	Mixed	Mixed	Private	Private	Public	Public
Germany	Mixed	Mixed	Mixed	Mixed	Private	Private	Mixed	Mixed
Ireland	Mixed	Mixed	Mixed	Mixed	Private	Private	Mixed	Mixed
Japan	Mixed	Private	Mixed	Mixed	Private	Private	Mixed	Private
New Zealand	Mixed	Mixed	Mixed	Mixed	Private	Private	Private	Private
Norway	Mixed	Mixed	Mixed	Mixed	Mixed	Mixed	Mixed	Mixed
Spain	Mixed	Mixed	Public	Public	Private	Private	Public	Mixed
Switzerland	Mixed	Mixed	Mixed	Mixed	Private	Private	Private	Private
Sweden	Mixed	Mixed	Mixed	Mixed	Mixed	Mixed	Mixed	Mixed
Turkey	Private	Private	Mixed	Mixed	Private	Private	Public	Mixed
United Kingdom	Public	Mixed	Mixed	Private	Mixed	Private	Public	Private
United States	Private	Private	Public	Public	Private	Private	Private	Private

Legend: Privately owned · Mixed · Publicly owned

65

London Bus Company restructured itself into 11 smaller units in 1989. London Regional Transport is also extending the procedure of competitive tendering of bus routes. Currently, 25 per cent of the network is operated by contractors and it is envisaged that 40 per cent of the network will be competitively tendered by 1992.

In Northern Ireland, prices for inter-city and local buses are not regulated but operators are required to pre-notify prices and fare changes to central government but no control is exercised over the notified fare levels. Also as regards entry to the market and regulation of services, application must be made for licences for individual routes. There is no cap on the number of firms but in practice most inter-city bus services in Northern Ireland are provided by the state-owned company, Ulsterbus (Citibus for local services). Operators may be required to provide services on certain uneconomic routes as a social service.

In Great Britain (except for London), prices for local bus services are now unregulated on commercial services except when subsidised by local authorities who may set the fares.

An extensive program of privatisation and dismemberment has also been undertaken recently. In 1988, the National Bus Company was split up into 72 operating companies and privatised. The Scottish Bus Corporation is also about to be privatised.

The 1985 Transport Act also ended the exemption from the competition legislation for the bus industry. Since then, 142 agreements between bus companies covering fares, market-sharing or timetables and routes, bus stops and livery have been registered.

Since then, the Office of Fair Trading (OFT) has undertaken several investigations into alleged anti-competitive practices by bus companies, particularly predatory pricing or other exclusionary behaviour. In 1987, following a complaint by a small bus operator on the Isle of Wight against the dominant operator, the latter's policy of denying other operators use of its bus station was deemed to restrict competition in that it prevented existing and prospective competitors from using an essential means of bringing their bus services to passengers' attention.

Two separate investigations were begun in 1988 into alleged predatory pricing by two Yorkshire bus companies and a further investigation into a bus company operating in the Inverness area.

Since deregulation the OFT has considered several mergers in the bus industry. Many of these have either not qualified for investigation under UK legislation or have been abandoned by the parties. Eight of these mergers have been referred to the Monopolies and Mergers Commission (MMC).

To date the MMC has published one report on such a merger. This found the acquisition by Badgerline Holdings of Midland Red West Holdings to be against the public interest. The Commission saw substantial benefits in the merger but considered that these were not sufficient to outweigh the detriments. The particular adverse effect was that the merger would weaken competitive tendering and thus increase the cost to Avon of supporting socially necessary bus services or make it impossible for Avon to support these services.

United States

Continuing the movement toward full deregulation of the surface transportation industry in the United States, Congress enacted the Surface Freight Forwarder Deregulation Act, Pub. L. No 99-521 in 1986. The law eliminates much federal and state economic regulation of surface freight forwarders (except for forwarders of household goods) and removes antitrust immunity for collective ratemaking by that segment of the transportation industry.

In October 1986, Congress authorised a public offering of the stock of Consolidated Rail Corporation ("Conrail") that had previously been held by the United States government. See 45 U.S.C. par. 1301, et seq. This legislation had the effect of privatizing Conrail, a major railroad in the eastern United States.

The Federal Trade Commission staff gave support to deregulating California's trucking industry in response to a request for comments from that state's Public Utilities Commission. The staff in its response stated, "the evidence is clear that trucking deregulation has been of great benefit to consumers wherever it has been tried. Consumers benefit from lower rates with no decline in service".

The Commission staff commented on a bill before the Ohio legislature which would take a major step in deregulating that state's trucking industry. The staff stated that the bill is "a significant step toward bringing to consumers the benefits of price competition in Ohio's motor freight industry". The staff noted that in California, partial deregulation of trucking from 1980 to 1986 resulted in lower rates with no loss in service.

The Commission staff, at the request of the Montgomery County, Maryland, Council, commented that deregulation of the taxicab business in Montgomery County would increase the number of taxis available to consumers, lower fares and increase employment opportunities. The staff suggested certain amendments to the proposed new taxicab law which would "let market forces determine both the number of cabs and the fares charged". The staff also noted that taxicab deregulation in Seattle, Washington, resulted in about 200 additional jobs and fares estimated to be 15 per cent lower than under regulated taxi service. In San Diego, California, after deregulation, the average waiting time for radio-dispatched cabs declined 20 percent.

In December 1989, the Department of Justice petitioned the Interstate Commerce Commission to revoke the collective ratemaking authority of Rocky Mountain Motor Tariff Bureau, a large rate conference of major motor carriers in the Western United States. The Department claimed that the Bureau was used by the carriers to collude unlawfully on parallel "independent action" increases, which the Commission does not regulate, rather than to formulate regulated "general rate increases".

European Communities

In 1988 and 1989, three main measures were taken in the road haulage industry.

Quantitative restrictions

Apart from the trade in certain types of goods and links between certain Member States, road haulage operations are subject to quotas for links between Member States. However, following a Council Regulation of 1988 on international intra-Community routes all quotas will be abolished by 1993. Hauliers will only have to satisfy qualitative conditions in order to have access to the Community market.

"Cabotage"

In December 1989, the Council adopted a regulation laying down the conditions under which non-resident carriers may operate national road haulage services within a Member State. This Regulation institutes a transitional regime for the years 1990, 1991 and 1992. Through a system of cabotage quotas, under certain conditions, any road haulier established in a Member State will be allowed, from 1 July 1990, to carry out national road haulage operations in a different Member State from the one in which he is established. In the event of a crisis due to the introduction of cabotage, the Commission is authorised to take any necessary measures.

Tariffs

In December 1989, the Council adopted a new Regulation on the fixing of rates for the carriage of goods by road between Member States. From 1 January 1990, these rates are governed by a system of rate-fixing by free agreement between the parties to the haulage contract.

B. Air

Australia

Domestic aviation

In October 1987, the government announced its decision to fully withdraw from the detailed economic regulation of domestic interstate aviation. However, as the terms of the airlines agreement require three years notice of termination, it is not possible to accomplish deregulation before 1990. In Australia, air traffic on the major national or trunk routes is largely reserved for two airlines as a result of long-standing agreement between the government and the two airlines in question (Ansett and Australian Airlines) since 1952. The agreement in turn is supported by a complex package of legislation which allows the government to control aircraft capacity and entry onto trunk routes, and the Independent Airfares Committee to set airfares. Domestic operators may be required to obtain state government approval of air fares where they propose to operate intra-state services. Requirements for the granting of fare approvals vary between states

Following 30 October 1990, foreign interests wishing to establish new firms, or to invest in existing firms, in the domestic aviation industry will be required to comply with

Foreign Investment Review Board guidelines. In addition, foreign airlines operating services to Australia will be limited to less than 15 per cent investment in any one domestic operator.

The Federal Government also regulates the domestic aviation industry in respect of safety and operational matters. Domestic operators may be required to obtain state government licences where they propose to operate intra-state services. Requirements for the granting of state licences vary between states.

In the post-1990 deregulated environment, the aviation industry will be fully exposed to the Trade Practices Act. Any move towards the emergence of market dominance by acquisition on the network of national routes would be dealt with by section 50 of the Act, which covers market dominance resulting from mergers. Other provisions of the Act would prevent abuses of market power, such as predatory pricing, and other anticompetitive practices.

Recent developments have been the lodgement of two applications with the Civil Aviation Authority for approval to operate domestic air routes following deregulation and 14 expressions of interest to the Federal Airports Corporation from other airlines seeking terminal space at airports. The Trade Practices Commission is examining the anticompetitive implications of computer reservation systems and restrictive leasing conditions both of airport space and holiday resorts serviced by regional airports.

Austria

A more liberal licensing system has been operated in recent years, and a fourth airline — Lauda Air — has been granted a licence to operate in competition with the existing airlines.

Canada

Under the National Transportation Act (NTA) which went into effect on 1st January 1988, air carriers are allowed to establish fares and fare decreases without regulatory discretion. However, fare increases on monopoly routes are appealable to the National Transportation Agency unless they form part of a confidential contract. In Northern Canada, following complaint action, air carriers may be subject to Agency review of both fare levels and increases. As concerns entry, beyond the reverse onus criteria in Northern Air markets, in Southern Canada "public convenience and necessity" entry criteria have been replaced by "fitness" criteria.

France

In 1987 and 1988, two sets of measures were adopted :

1. Liberalisation of the services between metropolitan France and the overseas departments, subject to the requirement that the operating companies observe public service obligations;

2. Experimental liberalisation of charter flights in metropolitan France subject to certain conditions being fulfilled;

3. Experimental double designation of regular French carriers or services to overseas territories (New Caledonia, Polynesia) and on international routes where market conditions allow (San Francisco).

Germany

Legislation provides for special regulation of the transport sector, exempting from the antitrust laws any restriction of competition by government-set rates and conditions. Furthermore, a number of special agreements are exempt from the ban on horizontal and vertical competition-impeding agreements; they are, however, subject to monitoring against abuse. The restrictions involved normally result from arrangements for air and ocean transport, shipping in coastal and inland water-ways, seaport and airport companies, collective shipment by forwarding agents, and co-operation among companies that transport passengers by road.

One of the aims of the fifth law amending the Cartel Act which became effective on 1st January 1990, was to reduce the number of exemptions, thus adapting German regulations to the superior EC rules governing transport markets. The exemptions from the ban on cartels provided for under German law are thus to be dropped for international ocean-going navigation that is subject to EC legislation, and for EC air transport. Exemptions for airport and seaport companies, as well as a number of insignificant exceptions, the need for which has not been shown, have also been eliminated.

Conditions on markets for international air transport have now changed as new carriers have been admitted to the market. In 1989, the Government decided to reduce the State interest in Deutsche Lufthansa to 54.22 per cent in the course of an increase in the corporation's share capital. Two private airlines, German Wings and Acro Lloyd, have begun to operate scheduled airline services in competition with Deutsche Lufthansa. In one competition enforcement case in the airline industry, the Federal Cartel Office prohibited the purchase of a regional airline company, Südavia, by the DLT, a subsidiary of Deutsche Lufthansa on the main grounds that the slots the company had at Munich airport would have fallen to DLT.

Ireland

Significant steps have been taken in Ireland in the promotion of a liberalised regime in the aviation sector. Charter policy has been fundamentally reviewed and tariff filing requirements for carriers have been simplified. A further review of charter policy is being undertaken. Existing regulation of the domestic market applies mainly to entry on a particular route. In practice, frequency, capacity etc. are not regulated. In March 1988, revised bilateral arrangements were concluded with the UK which include provisions in relation to fares, market access and an open capacity regime which are among the most liberal in Europe. Ireland is a strong proponent of further liberalisation in the air transport sector in Europe.

Japan

In December 1985 the regulatory framework known as the "Aviation Constitution" which determined the permissible level of competition between Japanese airlines was abolished with the aim of increasing competition both domestically and internationally. A double or triple track approach has been adopted to this end. In addition, in December 1987, Japan Air Lines was completely privatised.

New Zealand

Previously companies operating domestic air services were unable to have more than 24.9 per cent foreign ownership. In 1986 this was changed to 50 per cent and in 1988 the restriction was abolished. Air New Zealand was privatised in August 1989.

Norway

The regulation of domestic air freight ended on 1 September 1987 as a result of liberalisation of international air freight and deregulation of domestic road freight. Since 1987, the deregulation of air freight put an end to the obligations to transport and the regulation of prices by the government. Domestic freight charter will be allowed on the same terms as international freight charter.

Portugal

As regards air transport, some liberalisation of air fares has taken place with the authorities only intervening in relation to services with a significant social impact. The Minister of Transport is alone responsible for approving fares for international scheduled services. As regards the fares on domestic services between continental Portugal and Madeira and the Azores, these are partly fixed by the Minister of Transport and partly by all the responsible ministers, i.e. the Price Control Minister, the Minister of Transport and the Minister of Finance.

Spain

The process of liberalising air transport in Spain will be undertaken in accordance with the decisions taken by the EEC in its successive liberalising packages.

However, two differentiating elements should be mentioned in the existing Spanish air transport regulations. Neither take off or landing slots nor ground handling contracts are regulated. The air passenger transport subsector in the charter area is being liberalised in practice in relation to tariffs, entry and service. This fact takes on great significance when it is realised that charter traffic accounts for 75 per cent of international air passenger transport in Spain.

Sweden

Within the air transport sector, deregulation steps have been decided on within the uniform Scandinavian civil aviation policy (1987). The deregulation concerns mainly split cargo charter, express parcel services and some intra-Scandinavian services. However, maximum prices, entry and services remain regulated on domestic passenger services.

In 1988, the Competition Ombudsman wrote to the government to call attention to a prohibition within the air transport sector which prevents travel agencies from sharing their commission with their customers. This is an obstacle to price competition between travel agencies. It is not quite clear, though, if the prohibition is a part of the governmental regulation of air fares or if it is wholly dependent on agreements between airline companies. The Competition Ombudsman wants this to be clarified before considering further measures. At the beginning of 1989, the Competition Ombudsman sent a letter to the government suggesting different deregulation steps within the domestic airline system in Sweden. The National Price and Competition Board has also recommended that the government allow competition in the domestic airline system and the Board of Civil Aviation has suggested an investigation in the matter. The new Competition Committee has received instructions to look into different regulated sectors, i.e. air traffic regulation.

Turkey

Airline fares are regulated but entry to the market is not. As regards service regulation, only the capacity of firms is not regulated.

United Kingdom

The privatisations of British Airways (BA) and British Airport Authority (BAA) were completed in January 1987 and July 1987 respectively.

In 1985, the Director General of Fair Trading gained additional powers under the Fair Trading Act 1973 and the Competition Act 1980 in matters affecting airline competition. However, complaints about anti-competitive behaviour are usually considered first by the Civil Aviation Authority (CAA) which, when it finds that there is a case to be heard, will seek a decision from the Secretary of State.

In 1986, the CAA received an application from Britannia Airways designed to limit the participation of BA in the short-haul leisure market, particularly the inclusive tour charter market on the grounds that BA's size and strength, its domination of international scheduled services and its privileged position at Heathrow gave it the opportunity to exploit these advantages to compete unfairly with specialist charter airlines. The application was refused because the CAA concluded that there was insufficient evidence of anti-competitive behaviour.

Probably the most significant development in the application of competition law to airlines in the UK was the reference to the Monopolies and Mergers Commission (MMC) of the acquisition by British Airways plc of British Caledonian Group plc. In 1987, the MMC reported that the acquisition might be expected not to operate against the public interest. However, the MMC identified a number of possible detrimental effects of the acquisition, mostly relating to the dominant position occupied by the merged airline in the United Kingdom market. As a result, the MMC recommended that, inter alia, BA should return to the CAA a number of the licences and slots formerly held by BCal, although BA was allowed to re-apply for them. Subsequently, several new services were licensed from Gatwick, in particular by Air Europe, and, to a lesser extent, Dan-Air. (See also *Deregulation and Airline Competition*, OECD, 1988, page 48.)

The degree of regulation exercised over airline prices has been diminishing over a number of years and, under proposals to come into force shortly, fares will normally come into effect automatically once filed with the appropriate central body (the Civil Aviation Authority — CAA). Intervention will only be made, in virtually all instances, on competition criteria, i.e. that a price is predatory or excessively high.

There is no cap on the number of airlines operating domestic services, nor is there any government imposed control over frequency of flights, quality of services, type of equipment etc. Operators must obtain licences for individual services from the CAA and these are now normally granted. The CAA will, however, reject applications on occasion, for example when there are a number of applications and the evidence indicates that it would not be in the interests of customers to licence all airlines. Such rejections are far less frequent now than was the case 15 years ago.

United States

Allocation of takeoff and landing rights

In comments filed in response to a proposed Department of Transportation (DOT) and Federal Aviation Administration (FAA) rulemaking, the Antitrust Division in 1986 urged the use of market-based approaches to allocate takeoff and landing rights ("slots") at four congested airports. The Division suggested that the DOT remove unnecessary restrictions on the slot market and include slots currently held by commuter carriers and slots used for international air service to ensure the most efficient mix of operations. Subsequently, the FAA adopted final rules which required a market-based approach.

Similarly in 1987, the Federal Trade Commission's staff recommended to DOT that airlines not be granted immunity from the antitrust laws to discuss the allocation of takeoff and landing slots at certain major airports. Instead, the staff recommended that DOT should permit the airlines to buy and sell the slots to relieve congestion problems. The staff was concerned that the grant of immunity would facilitate anticompetitive agreements. A system of buying and selling slots, however, could be used to solve the congestion problems, as well as to make it easier for new competitors to enter the market.

Computer reservation system

In October 1988, the Department responded to a congressional request for its views concerning a recent DOT study of the Computer Reservation System ("CRS") industry. See DOT, *Study of Airline Computer Reservation Systems*, DOT P-37-88-2 (May 1988). The DOT study presented new evidence that supports the conclusion that dominant CRS vendors have market power; this evidence includes an apparent wide disparity between airline booking fees and the average unit cost of providing the service, and the persistence of substantial incremental revenues, despite DOT's rules prohibiting overt display bias. The DOT study also repeated concerns about certain clauses in travel agent subscriber contracts (e.g., roll-over provisions, liquidated damaged clauses, and minimum-use clauses) that tend to restrict the agents' ability to switch easily among vendors. In a letter to Senator Howard M. Metzenbaum, the Department discussed the DOT study and concluded that neither that study nor other evidence examined suggested probable violations of the antitrust laws that would warrant a new investigation by the Department. Although the Department concluded that the new evidence raised legitimate competitive issues and suggested that the dominant CRS providers continue to possess market power, the evidence was not sufficient to suggest that the vendors had engaged in the sort of "bad acts" that were required for a Sherman Act monopolisation violation. The Department observed that DOT's regulatory process (under its CRS rules) seemed sufficient to deal with any complaints about CRS at this time. However, the Department warned that even regulatory action against CRS providers should be approached with caution, because the only solution for supracompetitive pricing by the dominant vendors may be full-scale price regulation, a remedy that has proven to be costly and inefficient in other contexts.

In 1989, the Antitrust Division reviewed a proposed merger of American Airlines' Sabre CRS and Delta Airlines' Datas II. The carriers abandoned the transaction after the Division announced that it would sue under the antitrust laws to block it

In response to an advance notice of proposed rulemaking issued by the Department of Transportation, the Antitrust Division in November 1989 filed comments urging that the 1984 CRS rules be extended past their five year expiration. The Division also suggested consideration of other procompetitive rules, including pass-through of booking fees to passengers and restrictions on the terms vendors may require in subscriber contracts. The Division noted in its comments that if additional rules do not solve the competitive problems in the CRS industry, structural relief would be the only alternative.

Mergers

As of 1 January 1989, airline mergers and acquisitions that were formerly subject to regulatory approval by DOT under Section 408 of the Federal Aviation Act ("Act") are now subject only to enforcement of the antitrust laws by the Department of Justice. Another change on 1 January was the termination of DOT's authority under sections 412 and 414 of the Act (49 U.S.C. par. 1382 and 1384) to approve and immunise various intercarrier agreements. Henceforth, such intercarrier agreements must comply with the antitrust laws. Enforcement of section 411 of the Act (49 U.S.C. par. 1381), which prevents unfair and deceptive practices, is still the responsibility of DOT.

Over the period 1986-1988, the Antitrust Division intervened in a number of mergers being reviewed by the DOT. The Division did not oppose Texas Air Corp.'s acquisition of Eastern Airlines in light of Texas Air's agreement to sell to Pan American certain takeoff and landing rights at New York's La Guardia Airport and Washington's National Airport as well as gates at La Guardia and Boston's Logan Airport. The agreement resolved the Division's concerns arising from the acquisition's elimination of competition between

Eastern and New York Air, a Texas Air subsidiary. Prior to the acquisition, Eastern and New York Air were the only carriers operating high-frequency shuttle service between Washington, New York and Boston.

The Division was unsuccessful in opposing two other airline acquisitions that the Division argued would result in the elimination of competition in regional markets. Over the Division's objections, the DOT held that Northwest Airlines' purchase of Republic Airlines and Trans World Airlines' acquisition of Ozark Airlines did not substantially restrain competition despite the increase in concentration and the reduction in the number of carriers with "hub" operations in certain cities from two to one. In airline terminology, "hubs" are airports where particular airlines schedule a large number of arrivals at the same time, allowing passengers to make rapid connections to a wide choice of destinations.

The Division did not oppose the acquisition by Texas Air of People Express Airlines and the assets of Frontier Airlines, Inc., a wholly-owned subsidiary of People Express. The Division analysed the proposed acquisition of Frontier separately from the acquisition of People Express, concluding that the latter would not substantially lessen competition in certain city-pair routes and airport pairs in which Texas Air and People Express competed. Texas Air's acquisition of Frontier's jet fleet raised more difficult competition issues. However, the Division decided not to oppose the transaction in light of the fact that Frontier was in bankruptcy and in view of the DOT's decision to permit the Northwest-Republic and TWA-Ozark mergers, where the increase in concentration on certain city-pair routes was greater than the increase resulting from Texas Air's acquisition of Frontier.

In comments filed with the DOT, the Division supported the adoption of an expedited review process for airline mergers, but opposed the use of voting trust arrangements that would allow one airline to acquire substantial stock in another prior to any governmental review of the acquisition's probable competitive effects.

After sunset on 1 January 1989 of the Department of Transportation's authority to review airline mergers, all airline transactions became subject to antitrust scrutiny by the Department of Justice.

In June 1989, the Antitrust Division announced that it would sue to prevent the proposed sale by Eastern Airlines of a block of ten gates at Philadelphia International Airport to USAir, its chief rival at Philadelphia. Eastern instead sold the gates to Midway Airlines, which has since started a new hub to compete with USAir at Philadelphia.

EEC

Five identically worded references for a preliminary ruling made by the Paris police court afforded the Court of Justice in 1986 an opportunity to pronounce on the compatibility with the EEC Treaty, and in particular with the competition rules of the compulsory approval procedure laid down by French law for air tariffs.

The French Civil Aviation Code — like the relevant provisions of the other Member States — stipulates that air transport may be provided only by enterprises approved by the Minister for Civil Aviation. These enterprises must submit their tariffs to the Minister for approval. The approval of a tariff renders it binding on all traders selling tickets of the airline concerned in respect of the route specified in the application for approval. In international air transport, which is governed by a network of bilateral agreements between the interested States, it is normal practice for companies authorised to operate a certain route first of all to negotiate a common tariff within IATA and then to submit it to the authorities of the signatory States for approval. The question referred was raised in criminal proceedings against the executives of airlines and travel agencies who had been prosecuted for marketing air tickets at prices not ministerially approved or different from the approved prices.

The court held that the Treaty's competition rules are equally applicable to the air transport sector. This follows from the very wording of Article 74, the first article in the Title on transport, in which Member States are urged to pursue the objectives of the Treaty, including, therefore, that set out in Article 3(f), namely undistorted competition. It is borne out by other provisions of the Title on transport — Articles 61 and 77 — which presuppose that the competition rules apply to the transport sector whether or not a common transport policy has been established, and by the fact that there is no provision in the Treaty which, along the lines of Article 42 in the Chapter on agriculture, excludes the application of the competition rules to transport or makes it subject to a decision by the Council.

Following intensive negotiation during the first half of the year the Council reached agreement in principle at the end of June 1987 on a package of measures to increase competition in the civil aviation sector. The formal adoption of this package was delayed by a bilateral disagreement over the status of Gibraltar airport. Once, the two Member States concerned had resolved this issue the Council was able to proceed to the adoption of the measures on 14 December 1987. In view of the delay in implementation, the Council decided that the measures should enter into force at the earliest possible date, namely 1 January 1988.

The package is a first step towards the completion of the internal market in air transport. While Member States will remain competent for their bilateral relations in air transport, the scope for the exercise of their sovereignty in respect of relations between Member States has been substantially reduced by the various measures, in particular since the system whereby both governments must agree on fares, capacity and airline designation has now been breached and objective criteria must be henceforth respected. Thus, for capacity a Member State will only be able to act to maintain its airlines' capacity share if that share falls below 45 per cent (or, after 1 October 1989, 40 per cent) of the total capacity mounted on all services between two Member States. There is thus scope for additional competition between airlines. This scope is reinforced by the greater possibilities afforded to airlines to set their own fares and, in particular, to relate their fares to their own costs rather than to the fares of other carriers. Moreover, there is provision for automatic approval of certain discount and deep-discount fares. The fares directive lays down criteria which member States must respect in approving fares and provides for arbitration, whose results are binding on governments, in the event of a disagreement. Finally, possibilities are opened up for new carriers to come on to particular routes, both in the context of multiple designation on the main Community routes and of fifth freedom operations. New traffic rights are created between the major airports and the regional airports, and this creates new possibilities for competition between hubs on connecting services. These access provisions are particularly significant, since they increase the contestability of air transport markets. The empirical evidence suggests that it is the presence of a new competitor on a route (rather that the threat of his arrival) which makes the differences to the level of fares.

Coastal shipping

The inquiry into coastal shipping examined the concern that the reservation of coastal shipping to Australian seamen may have resulted in the under-utilisation of that mode of transport in the Australian domestic economy. The Industries Assistance Commission was given a reference in 1988 to examine the manner in which deregulation would operate in coastal shipping.

Canada

The Shipping Conference Exemption Act was passed in December of 1987. This Act includes provision for confidential contracts between shippers and shipping conferences, prohibits joint negotiations of inland rates for multi-modal transportation of goods, and prohibits anti-competitive action against non-conference carriers. The legislation retained the basic exemption for conferences from the Competition Act but narrowed the scope of the exemption in some areas.

Ireland

Ireland adheres to the principle of free and fair competition in international shipping. State policy has been to promote full commercial freedom of shipping, with the ships of all nations free to trade without restrictions to and from Irish ports. Accordingly, Ireland would view with concern any measures (e.g. cargo reservation) which amounts to a restriction of competition. Ireland's commitment to full freedom for shipping services accords with the shipping policy of the European Community. In this regard the Council of the Community adopted a Regulation (No. 4056/86) in December 1986 (together with a set of three other Regulations intended to meet the threat to Community shipping from Third Country protectionist practices). The Regulation lays down detailed rules for the application of Articles 85 and 86 of the Treaty of Rome to maritime transport (prohibiting restrictive practices and abuse of dominant position).

New Zealand

In 1987, the New Zealand Government passed the Shipping Act , which aims at introducing some measure of competition to the international outwards shipping market.

Norway

As of 1 January 1987, the licensing of routes system for the transport of goods by ship was abandoned and tariff approval abolished.

Spain

In 1986, maritime freight transport was liberalised in conformity with EEC measures, allowing a progressive reduction in the volume of cargo to be carried in Spanish ships and easier access to the market by foreign shipping.

United States

In February 1988, the Department of Justice filed comments at the Federal Maritime Commission ("FMC") urging the FMC to disavow any regulatory jurisdiction over cargo movements between foreign ports, even if U.S. domestic cargo is involved (e.g., Chicago-origin cargo routed via Vancouver, Canada, to Japan). In December 1988, the FMC issued a decision adopting the view advanced by the Department.

After receiving extensive petitions from the industry to reconsider this ruling, the FMC reaffirmed its decision. The issue has been appealed to the courts.

In 1989, the Court of Appeals in Washington, D.C. heard arguments on whether the Shipping Act of 1984 allows conferences to prohibit their members from using their right of independent action to offer loyalty contracts to individual shippers. The Department of Justice opposed the FMC before the Court, maintaining that the right of independent action could not be so constrained.

In November 1989, the FMC released its five-year report on the effects of the Shipping Act of 1984. The Federal Trade Commission submitted a reply; a reply by the Antitrust Division will also be submitted.

EEC

On 22 December 1986, the Council adopted four regulations in the maritime transport sector. Regulation No 4056/86 lays down detailed rules for the application of Articles 85 and 86 to maritime transport. A block exemption is granted in respect of liner conferences. Conditions and obligations are attached to the exemption to protect the interests of transport users. The block exemption will be withdrawn if outside competition is eliminated owing to acts of conferences, change of market conditions or to an act of a third State, but, in this last-mentioned case, only after negotiations with such a State. The Regulation entered into force on 1 July 1987.

The other three regulations concern the principle of freedom to provide services in maritime transport within the common market and between the Member States and third countries, unfair pricing practices in maritime transport and the co-ordination of measures to safeguard free access to cargoes in ocean trades.

The Council invited the Commission to consider whether it is necessary to submit proposals regarding competition in passenger transport, tramp shipping, consortia in liner shipping and agreements between transport users. The Commission has undertaken to report to the Council within a year on whether it is necessary to provide for block exemptions for passenger transport services and consortia in liner shipping. Meanwhile, any request for an individual exemption of an agreement relating to passenger transport services will be carefully examined to see whether the agreement contributes to the facilitation of services.

With respect to consortia, the Commission held a hearing in which the shipping industry and representatives of the Member States were heard. The objective was to clarify the replies to the questionnaire distributed by the Commission and to obtain additional information.

Shipowners represented by CAASE and CENSA met again with the Commission in December. It was agreed that further meetings should take place with the object of defining the concept of "consortium."

Since the Regulation entered into force, the Commission has since received a number of formal complaints. These concern:

a) Two agreements between the liner conferences serving the west- and east-bound North Atlantic trades and some of their major non-conference competitors in those trades in order to discuss and to agree upon freight rates, and one agreement among the members of the aforementioned conferences on pooling of cost on certain routes and for certain commodities. This agreement, however, has now been terminated.

b) Cargo reservations and restrictions of free access to, and operation in, trades between Europe and West and Central Africa for non-conference lines.

c) Action by a conference operating in the Europe-African Trades against one of its own members.

The Commission also received three applications for individual exemptions for passenger conference agreements operating between the UK and France, Ireland and the Netherlands respectively.

In 1988, the Commission continued its study of the issues raised by consortia in liner shipping with a view to making a report to the Council on the appropriateness of providing for a block exemption. In the course of this study discussions were held with representatives of shipowners and the industry made available to the Commission a small number of consortia agreements. The analysis of these agreements indicated that they contain both technical and commercial arrangements whose details and extent are subject to wide variation, some going little beyond technical aspects relating to fleet and terminal operations while others contain a full range of commercial arrangements, such as pooling, joint marketing, conference rights and inland operations.

In these circumstances and on the basis of the information currently in its possession, the Commission felt that a block exemption could not be forwarded to the Council. The Commission considered, nevertheless, that a number of clauses to be found in consortia agreements and involving essentially technical co-operation could normally be granted an exemption under Article 85(3), whereas other clauses would have to be examined on the merits of each case. The Commission informed the shipowners' and shippers' organisations, and the Member States, of these conclusions and drew their attention to the fact that it had received no applications for exemptions in respect of consortia agreements.

In the case of the complaints relating to access for non-conference lines to trades between Europe and West and Central Africa, the Community has taken coordinated action pursuant to Council Regulation No 4058/86 within the framework of the Lomé Convention. Negotiations in an expert group between the Community and the African States concerned resulted in an agreed report on general principles (including free access to trades for non-conference lines) which was submitted to the ACP-EEC Council of Ministers meeting in Mauritius in May. The Council took note of the report and instructed the experts to pursue their work and to establish modalities for implementation.

Postal and Telecommunications Services

Australia

In September 1987 the government initiated a wide-ranging review of telecommunications policy which included close scrutiny of the extent to which those services should be deregulated and made subject to competition.

A new framework for telecommunications services was announced by the government in its May 1988 Economic Statement. AUSTEL has been established to facilitate deregulatory reform in telecommunications.

As regards postal services, the prices of basic letter services are subject to price surveillance while in 1990 prices and entry conditions in parcel and courrier services were not regulated.

Austria

The terminal equipment market has been largely deregulated in Austria and telecommunications services have been liberalised. Thus many national and international services have been established using the public networks.

Belgium

In connection with the EEC liberalisation initiatives (see below) a number of measures have been proposed to reform the regulatory system in telecommunications and will be submitted shortly to Parliament. The T. T. State-owned Corporation will remain the sole supplier of the basic network of services (the transmission and switching equipment comprising this network: telephone network, tele and data transmission) except for networks set up by private transmission and switching facilities not owned by the T. T. and except for the simple resale of rented national and international circuits. Private parties will thus be allowed to rent lines in order to create value-added networks.

The State-owned Corporation has a monopoly of three basic services: telephone (including mobile radio telephone services and radio paging), telex and data transmission but not including the supply of terminal equipment and modems. All other services — including so-called value added services — will be opened up to competition and in principle entry will be free on condition that the new services do not compete with the basic services.

The Corporation will however not be limited to providing basic services but will also offer services based on the use of complementary equipment and software such as telefax, teletext, videotex, electronic payment and mail and message services.

The supply of terminal equipment to customers will also be liberalised progressively in the near future in response to the increased choice offered to customers as a result of opening the market up to competition. Several types of equipment have already been liberalised: additional telephone sets, cordless telephones; additional teleprinters and special teleprinters, telematic terminal equipment: telefax, teletex and videotex machines; certain modems; and radio paging and mobile telephone terminal equipment. This liberalisation will be extended by 1991 to low capacity PABXs, other types of modems, the first telephone set and teleprinter and terrestrial receiving stations.

As has been the case up to now, the different types of equipment will be subject to approval before connection to the network. However approval of private terminal equipment will be exercised by a separate ministerial body and not by the T. T. Corporation as at present.

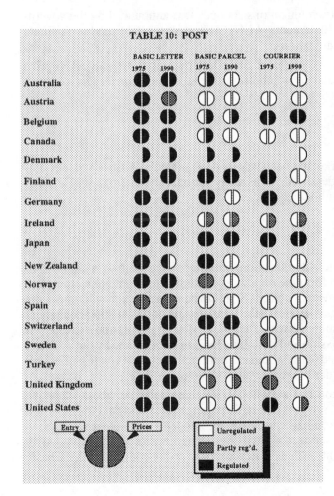

TABLE 10: POST

Canada

In October 1986, an intergovernmental inquiry published its report on telecommunication pricing and the universality of basic telephone service. This work continues to be used in the development of telecommunications policy and in the regulatory activities of the Canadian Radio-television and Telecommunications Commission (CRTC). The federal-provincial task force report on public long distance service competition was released in December 1988. This study examines other countries' experiences in public long distance competition and through empirical analysis investigates competitive alternatives to the existing structure. While not conclusive, the report will help form the basis of federal and provincial governments' policy on public long distance competition.

As regards the postal sector, prices and entry are regulated in the basic letter segment of the market but are unregulated as regards parcels and courrier services at the federal level. Entry to the parcel services sector is however provincially regulated. In the telecommunications sector, the prices of customer equipment and entry to the manufacture of such equipment are regulated in some Canadian provinces. In three provinces, state monopolies exist for all postal and telecommunication services.

Denmark

Basic telecommunication services in Denmark are divided between four regional concessionary monopoly-enterprises majority-owned by state or local government and Telecom Denmark, a state-owned enterprise responsible for all international services and certain inland services.

As a consequence of the ongoing process of liberalisation, customer equipment will be completely liberalised by 1st July 1990.

Finland

The conditions of competition in the field of telecommunications are controlled by the Ministry of Communications and by the Center for Telecommunications Administration. As to specific legislation applicable, two pieces of legislation are relevant: the Act on Telecommunications and the Act on Administration in the field of Telecommunications. The legislation concerning telecommunications has been reformed recently.

The Office of Free Competition is in a position to affect the conditions of competition in the field of telecommunications by taking initiatives for the Ministry of Communications to increase competition. On the other hand, the principles of free competition are reflected in the recent government policy on liberalising, e.g. trade in telecommunication equipment.

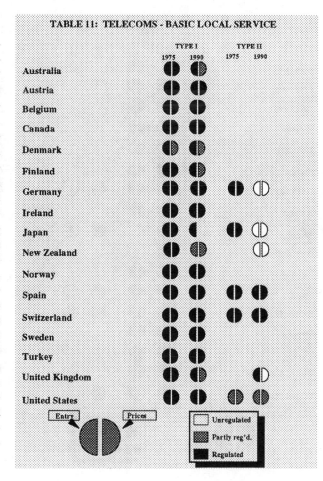

TABLE 11: TELECOMS - BASIC LOCAL SERVICE

85

France

Since 1987, the French government has taken three types of measure designed to open up the telecommunications sector:

— As regards value added services, any enterprise may now operate such services subject to notification to the Ministry of Posts and Telecommunications or to authorisation for firms wishing to operate large-scale networks;

— As regards mobile telephone systems, two operators have been authorised: France Télécom and the Compagnie Générale des Eaux;

— As regards radio paging services, there are two operators competing for this market: France Télécom and Télédiffusion de France.

Germany

In the Federal Republic of Germany, the commission set up to study the postal and telecommunications systems submitted its final report in 1987. Using this as a basis, the federal government presented a bill to parliament in 1988 providing for a restructuring of these systems. The Bundestag and Bundesrat have since passed the bill which went into effect on 1 July 1989. The Deutsche Bundespost has been split up into three independent companies dealing with postal services, banking and telecommunications, respectively. On the telecommunications side, the restructuring limits the Deutsche Bundespost's previous monopoly to its network and to voice transmission while expanding competition in telecommunications and terminal equipment. In addition, private parties are permitted to develop their own transmission networks for mobile and satellite communications. This should produce competition among the various networks.

As regards the current amount of regulation of postal services, prices and entry are

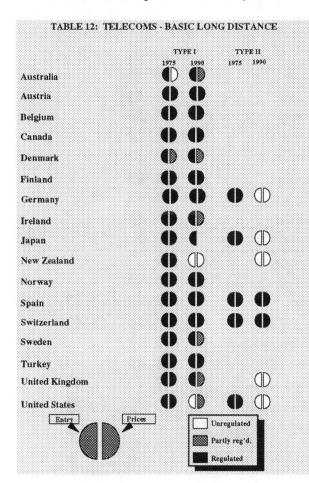

TABLE 12: TELECOMS - BASIC LONG DISTANCE

regulated for the letter service but not for parcel and courrier services. For telephone services, prices and entry are regulated for terrestrial networks and partly regulated for mobile and satellite networks. Value-added services and customer equipment are generally not regulated or partially regulated.

Ireland

Prior to 1 January 1984, telecommunications were run as a government service for which the Department of Posts and Telegraphs was responsible. Under the Postal and Telecommunications Services Act, 1983 (the 1983 Act) two separate commercial semi-State companies were set up to run the postal and telecommunications services and were granted exclusive privileges in their respective areas. The new companies, which were vested on 1 January 1984, are Telecom Eireann (TE) and An Post. They deal with telecommunications and postal services respectively.

Originally the 1983 Act contained provisions which exempted the exercise, by the two companies, of their exclusive privileges from competition legislation. This exemption was removed upon enactment of the Restrictive Practices (Amendment) Act, 1987. Thus the Restrictive Practices Acts, 1972 and 1987, and the Mergers, Takeovers and Monopolies (Control) Acts, 1978 and 1987, now apply to all activities of TE and An Post.

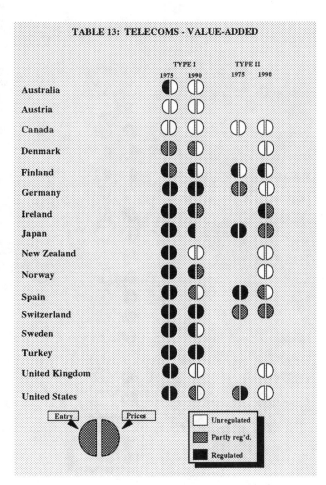

An Post has a monopoly on the delivery of letters and postcards but not on parcel or courrier services where it competes with private operators. It is required to obtain the prior approval of the Minister for Communications for all tariff increases whether the service is within or outside the postal monopoly. Private operators do not require such approval.

TE's exclusive privilege comprehends the provision of public telecommunications networks and services within the State. It does not comprehend international services but the company is licensed by the Min-

87

ister for Communications to provide international services. The Minister has also licensed An Post to provide national and international electronic mail services. Further liberalisation of the telecommunications services market is under consideration.

The telecommunications terminal equipment market has gradually been opened to competition since 1981. Only the market for first telephone sets is still restricted to the network operator, TE. However, this sector of the market will be opened to competition early in 1990.

Japan

A major reform of telecommunications occurred in 1985 when the monopoly provider of telecommunications services, Nippon Telegraph and Telephone Corporation (NTT) was privatised and subjected to considerable competition in all segments of the market. The legislation makes a fundamental distinction between type I and type II businesses; the former provide basic services over their own installed circuits and the latter offer enhanced services over circuits leased from type I operators.

Since deregulation and privatisation a large number of new enterprises have entered both types of business. At the end of 1988 the number entering type I business was 45 while the number offering mainly enhanced services (type II) amounted to 693.

The effect of the measures taken has been a lowering of price and a greater diversity of services with the concern being to ensure fair and effective competition between NTT and the new entrants.

New Zealand

Telecommunications

Formerly the Post Office carried out trading operations in banking, postal and telecommunications markets and had regulatory responsibilities under various statutes. Three state-owned corporations were created including Telecom Corporation to operate the telecommunica-

TABLE 14: TELECOMS - CUSTOMER EQUIPMENT

	1975	1990
Australia		
Austria		
Canada		
Denmark		
Finland		
Germany		
Ireland		
Japan		
New Zealand		
Norway		
Spain		
Switzerland		
Sweden		
Turkey		
United Kingdom		
United States		

Entry — Prices

Unregulated
Partly reg'd.
Regulated

tions trading activities. The Telecom Corporation was sold to a consortium led by Ameritech and Belt Atlantic of the United States in September 1990.

Telecom's statutory monopolies on customer premises equipment and public switched network services were abolished in 1988 and 1989 respectively. Since the sale of Telecom another company has commenced basic long-distance services so that as from September 1990 ownership of telecommunications service providers is largely private.

Postal Services

In 1988 the government reviewed the statutory monopoly held by the state-owned enterprise, New Zealand Post Ltd, on the basic letter post. It is to be retained for social policy reasons and the company will be required to comply with a deed of understanding in relation to universal price and rural service undertakings. The extent of the monopoly is to be reduced through changes to the definition of basic letter post.

Norway

On 1 January 1988 TBK, the subsidiary of the Norwegian Telecommunication Administration (NTA) responsible for equipment on customers' premises (CPE), was made a separate limited company fully owned by NTA. From the same date private companies were allowed to enter the market for CPE in competition with the TBK. To ensure fair competition the certifying of equipment was delegated to an independent organisation, Statens Teleforvaltning.

Portugal

The telecommunications sector has undergone profound changes in recent years and other reforms are in prospect. In 1987, Decree-Law

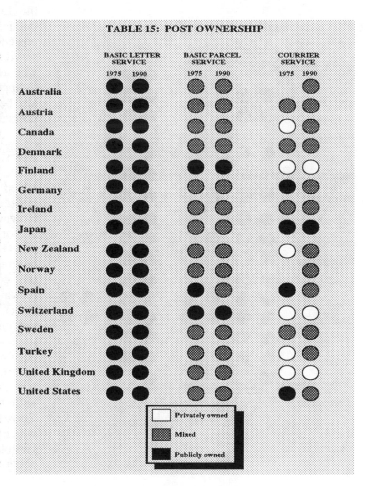

TABLE 15: POST OWNERSHIP

89

No. 355 of 14 November allowed greater flexibility in the fixing of prices and services offered by telecommunications operators. In particular, the Law distinguished between basic services and value-added services where competition should be encouraged.

A further Decree Law of 21 November 1988 established the rules for the approval of telecommunications terminal equipment.

Spain

Spanish legislation in force limits the monopoly of the postal administration to letters and post cards in an interurban context. The remaining activities, that is, all urban services and interurban services for newspapers, printed matter, business mail, samples, parcels, etc. are provided under conditions of free competition in which both private courier and parcel companies and the postal administration take part.

In Spain there is no distinction between companies of type I and II.

Since the entry in force of the law regulating telecom—munications in 1987, a system of posted tariffs for value added services has been established which the government is obliged to approve. These tariffs must also be sent to the associations of users and consumers.

With respect to entry, this Law stipulates that the provision of the greater part of the value-added services will be supplied under conditions of competition. However, prior administrative authorisation will have to be applied for, which is considered to be granted if within one month the government has not put forward any objection. Circumstances which may cause authorisation to be denied relate only to insolvency, technical inadequacy or lack of guarantees concerning the provision of the service under the conditions or with the necessary continuity. Those value added services which involve the use of non-switched telecommunication networks must, however, obtain

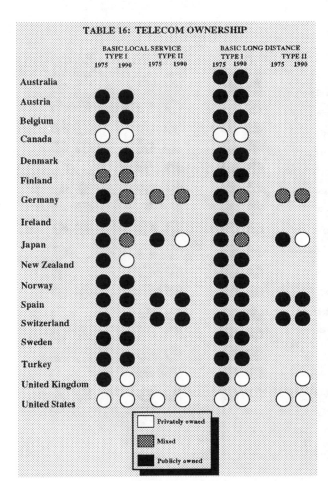

TABLE 16: TELECOM OWNERSHIP

temporary administrative authorisation which specifies the geographical area, the frequency (frequencies), power and other technical parameters.

At the present time the process of liberalisation of technical equipment is underway under the framework regulation for the effective liberalisation of second handsets and all additional equipment that can be connected to the network. At present, this process affects only additional equipment and second handsets; it is planned to extend it to digital exchanges in the short term and to the main telephone by the end of 1991. The only requirements which the liberalised product lines must comply with are the approved technical characteristics for approval.

Until liberalisation, the supply of telephone equipment was in the hands of a small number of private companies, in some of which the State-owned firm Telefonica S.A. had a holding. After gradual liberalisation many other companies, usually manufacturers of white or brown line electrical consumer goods, are beginning to produce telephones and other equipment connectable to the basic network.

Sweden

The National Telecommunication Administration (NTA) in Sweden administers the state owned network. Earlier NTA also had a monopoly on all equipment connected to the public network. During the 1980s more and more equipment has been opened up to competition and from 1 July 1989, the equipment market was completely deregulated. The technical specifications for equipment connected to the public network are still decided by NTA. From 1 January 1990, this task however will be transferred to a new government authority.

The deregulation of the telecommunication area also includes network services. NTA has declared that so called "third party traffic" on leased lines will be allowed in the near future. A working party, including a representa-

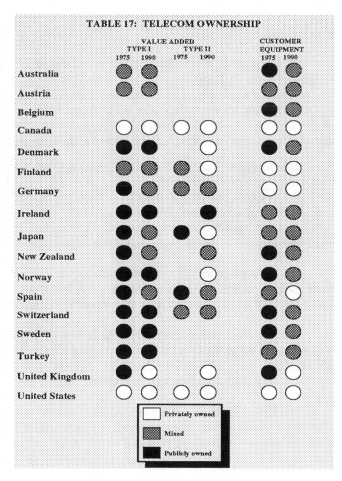

TABLE 17: TELECOM OWNERSHIP

	VALUE ADDED TYPE I		TYPE II		CUSTOMER EQUIPMENT	
	1975	1990	1975	1990	1975	1990
Australia	▨	▨			●	▨
Austria	▨	▨			▨	▨
Belgium					●	▨
Canada	○	○	○	○	○	○
Denmark	●	●		○	●	▨
Finland	▨	○	▨	○	○	○
Germany	●	▨	▨	▨	○	○
Ireland	●	●		●	▨	▨
Japan	●	▨	●	○	▨	▨
New Zealand	●	▨		▨	●	▨
Norway	●	●		○	●	▨
Spain	●	▨	●	▨	▨	○
Switzerland	●	●	▨	▨	●	▨
Sweden	●	●			●	▨
Turkey	●	●			●	●
United Kingdom	●	○		○	●	○
United States	○	○	○	○	○	○

○ Privately owned
▨ Mixed
● Publicly owned

91

tive of the Competition Ombudsman, has recently been set up by the government to discuss the terms for such traffic.

In the beginning of the 1980s the private company Comvik AB was permitted by the government to offer mobile telephone services in competition with NTA. In 1988 the government permitted Comvik to establish a new mobile telephone net according to the European GSM-system as well as a satellite connection between Sweden and North America. Comvik's applications were in both cases supported by the Competition Ombudsman.

The Sweden Post (SP) has traditionally been more exposed to competition than NTA. The only service which SP has a legal monopoly on is distribution of letters. The letter monopoly has however not been upheld by SP for the last 10-15 years. SP has also asked the government to abolish this monopoly.

In order to prevent cross-subsidizing between the monopoly and the competitive sector the NTA in 1981 was ordered by the Parliament to keep a separate account of the competitive sector. A few years later a similar obligation, at the Competition Ombudsman's request, was put on SP.

Switzerland

In December 1987, the Swiss government transmitted a draft of a new telecommunications act to the Parliament for deliberation. This act is to replace the existing law of 1922. The purpose of the law is to guarantee that the telecommunication needs of the population and the economy are met efficiently at a reasonable price and on an equal basis in all parts of the country. The law regulates the individual communications and makes a systematic distinction between the services, the network and user equipment.

The services are classified into basic services (consisting of transmission and switching of information on a telecommunications network) and enhanced services. While the basic service is reserved to the PTT and no private party is allowed to provide it to the public, all the other services can be provided by anyone, also on leased lines which may be connected to the public switched network. They include inquiry and information services, store-and-forward services, ciphering services and other information processing services.

The network monopoly will be maintained. If the PTT is not able to meet a third party's requirements in telecommunication infrastructure with its basic service (including leased lines), the third party is allowed to operate its own network on the basis of a licence.

The draft foresees a complete liberalisation of the market for user equipment, even if the opening-up of this market is carried out gradually in order to take due account of the liberalisation steps of foreign countries. In order to respect international standards however, only type-approved equipment will be available on the market.

The PTT will not be allowed to use its earnings from its monopoly activity to reduce the price of goods and services it provides in competition with third parties. A consultative commission with representatives of the interested parties will be created to advise the government on its decisions regarding telecommunications.

United Kingdom

Prior to 1981, the Post Office had a total monopoly of basic letter services. In 1981, this monopoly was changed to the extent that only letters when the service costs less than £1 remain as a post office monopoly. Otherwise courrier services in the United Kingdom are not subject to regulation. As regards parcels, the Post Office has never had a monopoly of parcels services but is a substantial force in the market. Its prices are regulated but prices for other private carriers are completely unregulated.

Since the 1986 report the UK has continued its policy of promoting effective competition at all levels in telecommunications markets. The UK has continued liberalisation in networks, service provision, and apparatus supply, and has enabled new services to be offered. Mercury Communications has continued to develop its all digital network. This now reaches more than 75 towns and cities, and its Mercury 2300 service for residential and single line business users is available to more than 50 per cent of the population of Great Britain. The competing cellular mobile radio operators have shown rapid expansion, between them having over 500 000 subscribers, making the UK the largest cellular market in the European Community. There has also been rapid development in paging, where the competing companies currently have over 580 000 subscribers. In services the UK now has the most liberal and open market in Europe. By 1987 over 200 operators were able to offer some 800 services, ranging from videotex and conference calls to electronic mail and retrieval systems. In that year the class licences for VADS and Branch Systems (which covers most systems run by individuals or companies within their own premises) were major steps in liberalisation and deregulation, taking over 99 per cent of operators out of the licensing procedures. With regard to apparatus, by the end of 1988 some 8 500 items of subscriber terminal equipment had been approved for general use.

Within the licensing and regulatory framework established under the Telecommunications Act 1984 the UK has proceeded in a liberalising and enabling fashion, promoting competition whilst safeguarding the integrity of the telecommunications networks. With regard to existing licences, in October 1985 the Director General of Telecommunications published his determination on the terms of interconnection between the Mercury and BT networks to ensure full network interconnection of the fixed link operators. A further illustration of the development of a competitive telecommunications environment was the Director General's decision in March 1988 that BT was obliged by its licence to provide connection services to independent satellite operators such as PanAmSat.

A number of new operators have been licensed since 1985. These include the awards in 1986 of licences to two competing operators of nationwide private mobile radio networks (PMR), as well as to London and regional PMR operators, and to operators of national paging networks. In 1988 six specialised satellite service licensees, in addition to BT, Mercury and Kingston Communications, were announced to provide specialist services to third parties via satellite. In January 1989 the Secretary of State for Trade and Industry announced the award of four licences to offer the new Telepoint services, which is expected to be offered on a commercial basis during 1989.

The regulation of, and promotion of competition in, the telecommunications sector is the responsibility of the Director General of Telecommunications and his office, OFTEL. OFTEL's powers and duties are set out in the Telecommunications Act 1984, the Competition Act 1980, and the Fair Trading Act 1973, and in the licences issued to public telecommunications operators (PTOs) and others. Much of OFTEL's work is concerned with the enforcement of the conditions in these licences, particularly that issued to the dominant operator, British Telecommunications plc (BT). The Director General is responsible for investigating complaints made to him and for answering representations about the conduct of PTOs. The total volume of complaints was at a very high level in 1988. These complaints relate to both competition and consumer issues.

Under the terms of its licence BT has to keep the average charge in the prices of its main telephone services within a figure set by the formula RPI-3 (so that if the Retail Price Index increases by 5 per cent, the average increase in telephone prices may be no more than 2 per cent). This provision is due to end in July 1989 and, following the publication of a consultative document, the Director General concluded that a further period of price control was justified. In July 1988 he announced that he had agreed with BT that the company would accept a very slight widening of the basket of services covered by the price control formula, and a new and tighter formula of RPI - 4.5. Within this overall ceiling BT has agreed to keep the annual increase in exchange line rentals below a cap of RPI+2.

In March 1988, the Director General announced that he had reached agreement in principle with BT that it would amend its contract for telephone service so as to accept limited liability, from April 1989, for failure to meet installation targets or when faults went unrepaired for more than a few days. OFTEL intends to seek similar improvements in BT's contracts for other services where competition is limited.

In 1988 there was significant progress in the development of competition in payphone services. Following a determination by the Director General in 1987 Mercury, the other main provider of network services, commenced the provision of public callbox services in July 1988. Also during 1988 OFTEL published a standard against which manufacturers could have payphones approved, so that customers could buy payphones for use on their premises rather than having to rent them from BT. OFTEL also established that, subject to agreement with the occupiers, firms were permitted to provide a "chain" of payphones on private premises, even though they did not occupy the premises.

In October 1988 the Department of Trade and Industry issued six licences to firms to operate specialised satellite services — these licences cover one-way point to multipoint services. This followed a separate earlier decision by the Director General which obliged BT to provide customers in the UK with circuits between the UK and a satellite operated by PanAmSat, and to convey messages in both directions over those links. PanAmSat, if its arrangements proceed according to plan, will operate the first privately owned satellite to provide international service.

Following a review carried out in 1988, the Director General concluded that a cap on the level of purchases which BT could make from Mitel Corporation (part of the undertakings given by BT following an adverse report by the MMC in 1986 on the proposed acquisition by BT of 51 per cent of Mitel) should not be lifted from 1 January 1989. Whether it should be modified or removed at a future date is a subject for review by the Office of Fair Trading.

In July 1988 OFTEL made its first reference to the MMC, asking it to investigate chatline and message services. The Monopolies and Mergers Commission's report on these services was published in February 1989. It concluded that the provision by BT of chatline and message services by means of its public switched telephone network, and the provision by BT of a telecommunications service to other persons enabling them to provide chatline and message services by means of its public switched telephone network, operated or might be expected to operate against the public interest in that, due to the ease of access to the services and the terms of contract between BT and its customers, the customer had inadequate control over the types of service which could be accessed and over the costs or charges that might be incurred for the use of the services, which significantly impaired the value and quality of the telephone service to the customer. The report suggested modifications to BT's licence which could remedy or prevent the adverse effects on the public interest identified by the Commission.

OFTEL has also considered a number of other issues relating to premium rate recorded message services provided over BT's telephone network, following complaints from both customers and independent service providers competing with BT. Some of the complaints proved justified; assurances were sought from BT that the matters would be remedied and in one instance the Director General issued a determination that BT was infringing the condition of its licence which prohibits it from showing undue preference to, or exercising undue discrimination against, particular persons or groups. BT immediately took steps to remedy the position.

During the first half of 1989 OFTEL conducted a review of the rules governing the restrictions on the use of private circuits. These were contained in the Branch Systems General (BSGL) and Value Added and Data Services (VADS) licences. As a result of this review, advice was given by the Director General of Telecommunications to the Secretary of State that the use of private circuits should be liberalised. One major effect of this action will be to allow the simple resale of capacity on private circuits. International simple resale will continue to be prohibited, but the Director General has said that he will keep this matter under review, and the new licence will allow for the liberalisation of international private circuits on a piecemeal basis.

The Director General also gave advice to the Secretary of State with regard to the licensing of new operators for personal communication network (PCN) services and for Telepoint. The Secretary of State subsequently announced four licensees for Telepoint, taking into account the Director General's advice, and he also announced that Mercury would receive a PCN licence subject to a sound application being presented. The Secretary of State further stated that he was inviting applications for an additional one or two licences for PCN operators.

The Director General in 1989 launched an investigation into the quality of service on the two competing cellular networks, Racal Vodafone and Cellnet, which is partly owned by British Telecom (BT). This action was in response to a large number of complaints from users about the quality of service on these systems.

In 1989 the Director General also launched an investigation into the future of numbering for telephony services. He issued a consultative document in July 1989, welcoming suggestions and comments from users. The impact of alternative numbering schemes on the development of competition was to be an important consideration in evaluating the possible options.

In 1989 the Director General was asked to settle the terms under which BT and Mercury should interconnect for access to premium rate services. The telephony interconnect agreement of 1985 did not lay down the terms under which the customers of one company should be able to access the service providers on the other company's network. The Director General investigated the costs of the parties, and made a determination for BT and Mercury to incorporate into a commercial agreement.

United States

The AT&T consent decree was agreed to by the United States and AT&T and approved by the court in 1982 to settle a major government antitrust case. In that case, the United States had alleged that AT&T illegally used its monopoly power in local exchange telephone service markets to exclude competition in the telecommunications equipment and interexchange ("long-distance") services markets. To remedy and prevent recurrence of that anticompetitive conduct, the decree required AT&T to divest the Bell Operating Companies ("BOCs") of their monopolies on local telephone service, and it prohibited the BOCs from providing interexchange services or information services, from manufacturing or providing telecommunications equipment or manufacturing customer premises equipment ("CPE"), and from providing any other product or service except exchange telephone service and "yellow pages" directories. The decree also contains provisions prohibiting anticompetitive discrimination by the BOCs. At the court's instance the parties included in the decree a provision for removal or waiver of the line-of-business restrictions by the court "upon a showing by the petitioning BOC that there is no substantial possibility that it could use its monopoly power to impede competition in the market it seeks to enter".

In 1987, after conducting its first general review of the decree restrictions, the Department of Justice recommended that the court lift the restrictions on BOC participation in information services, manufacturing, and non-telecommunications businesses, but that it retain the general interexchange restriction, subject to the waiver process. The BOCs sought removal of all the decree restrictions. There was substantial industry opposition to these requests. Judge Greene removed the restriction on non-telecommunications activities, modified the information services restriction to allow the BOCs to provide certain transmission-related "gateway" and storage and retrieval services, and denied all other requests for lifting of the restrictions. Appeals from that decision are pending in the DC Circuit. The United States contends that the district court based its decision on an incorrect legal standard and asks the court of appeals to reverse and remand the decision insofar as it denied the motions for removal of the information services and manufacturing restrictions. The appeal was argued in December 1989 and a decision is expected in 1990.

Throughout the period, the Antitrust Division continued its active role in the US telecommunications market, which was partially deregulated during the 1980s. For example, in 1986 the Division filed comments with the Federal Communications Commission (FCC) opposing its adoption of proposed "must-carry" rules that, with certain limitations, would have required cable operators to carry broadcast television signals. The Division argued that the proposed rules would impose significant restrictions on cable operators' programming decisions and raise Constitutional freedom of speech concerns. The FCC adopted the rules, but they were declared unconstitutional.

In 1987, the Division filed comments concerning a proposal by the FCC to reduce regulation of certain basic telecommunications services, specifically: (1) "packet-switched" data transmission services and telecommunications services and (2) systems provided under contracts awarded pursuant to competitive bidding. ("Packet switching" technology employs bursts of data to transmit digital information for terminal-to-terminal, terminal-to-computer, and computer-to-computer communications.) The Division generally supported the FCC's efforts to deregulate basic telecommunications services where such services are offered competitively. The Division thus agreed with an FCC proposal to streamline the regulation of packet-switched services, provided that safeguards are put into place to prevent anticompetitive discrimination and cross-subsidization. The Division also urged the FCC to consider full deregulation of packet-switched services once such safeguards are in place. Conversely, the Division argued that it would be premature to substitute competitive bidding for price regulation of services provided by the regional BOCs created under the 1982 AT&T consent decree. The Division noted that the BOCs retained bottleneck control in many cases over the services or facilities they offered. By the end of 1987, the FCC had not acted on its proposals.

The Division also filed comments on a major FCC proposal to compare the costs and benefits of "price-cap" ratemaking for various telecommunications services to the current system of rate-of-return ratemaking for AT&T and the BOCs. (Generally speaking, "rate-of-return" ratemaking is based upon a carrier's costs of service, including a reasonable profit. By contrast, "price-cap" ratemaking sets maximum limits on rates regardless of the carrier's costs.) The Division's comments also addressed the question of whether continued price regulation of any type was required for particular services. With respect to long-distance service, the Division argued that available evidence did not warrant the conclusion that such service was likely to give rise to a natural monopoly. Based on that conclusion, and on the fact that AT&T now faced significant competition for most of its services, the Division urged the FCC immediately to deregulate most AT&T services or to adopt streamlined ratemaking regulation. In those services markets in which AT&T did not face substantial competition (as in toll-free long-distance service and in some international long-distance markets), the Division argued that continued ratemaking regulation might be necessary for a relatively short period and that, in these circumstances, price-cap ratemaking appeared to be superior to rate-of-return ratemaking. According to the Division, that was because a properly set price-cap could eliminate the incentive to cross-subsidize, through misallocation of costs, that arises when a firm, such as AT&T, provides both regulated monopoly and unregulated competitive services. Furthermore, the Division added, a price-cap may reduce both the direct costs of regulation and a carrier's incentive to overinvest in its rate base.

The Division's "price-cap" comments also addressed ratemaking in connection with the BOCs. The Division noted that although AT&T was subject to increasing competition in most of its services markets, it was impossible to predict when the BOCs would lose their local telephone service monopolies. Thus, the Division argued, ratemaking regulation for the BOCs was likely to be required for some time. Because the disadvantages of price-cap ratemaking, such as the risk of quality degradation, are significantly enhanced where such regulation is in place for long periods of time, the Division suggested that price-cap regulation should not be applied to the BOCs pending further study. After further proceedings, the FCC adopted a modified form of price-cap regulation for AT&T and is considering some form of price-cap regulation for the BOCs.

In various FCC proceedings related to charges for access to local telephone exchange facilities, the Division urged the Commission to refine these charges so that competing services are treated equally. The Division also urged the Commission to promote efficient use of the network and deter uneconomic "bypass" of the local exchange by recovering non-traffic-sensitive costs through fixed, rather than usage-based, charges.

Postal services

In two filings before the US postal service (USPS), the Division supported regulations to permit international remail services. Remailers ship bulk mail, such as catalogues and magazines, from the United States to those foreign postal authorities that offer to reship the materials to their destination at the best combination of service and price. The Division argued that efficiencies would be enhanced if private firms were permitted to compete with the USPS in international mail routes and questioned the USPS's authority to restrict such competition. The USPS ultimately agreed with the Division and issued regulations that permitted private remail services. In December 1989, the Court of Appeals for the District of Columbia Circuit held that USPS acted arbitrarily and capriciously in adopting these regulations, because USPS failed to consider the impact of the regulation on all of USPS's patrons and failed to explain why narrower regulations were rejected. The Court of Appeals decision allows USPS to reconsider these issues.

In 1988, the Department undertook a study of whether the public interest would be served by increasing competition in providing postal services and, if so, how this goal might be best achieved (for example, by privatising certain functions in the USPS or by permitting private firms to compete with USPS). The study will address what reforms would ensure that postal service is supplied to the public at the lowest possible cost, consistent with other goals, such as adequate protection for USPS employees and maintenance of adequate service in rural areas. The Department hopes to complete this study during 1990.

EEC

On 16 May 1988 (OJ L 131, 27.5.1988, p. 73) the Commission adopted a Directive based on Article 90 of the EEC Treaty which requires Member States to establish a system of free competition in the Community market for telecommunications terminal equipment, and in particular, for telephone sets, modems and telex terminals.

These markets have hitherto been partitioned, with most Member States reserving for their national administrations the exclusive right to import, to market certain services, to make connections to the public network or to provide maintenance. The directive therefore requires the abolition of these exclusive rights which infringe Treaty rules. In addition, because the technical characteristics of the networks in the 12 Member States are very different, the Member States are required to publish these so that producers in other Member States can adapt their terminal equipment to the characteristics of each telecommunications network. The Member States are also required to vest the powers, held by the national telecommunications administrations, to adopt technical specifications and type-approval procedures, in an independent entity. This is because, as matters stand, the administrations are economic operators able, by virtue of those powers, to remove competing products from the market. Finally, the Directive requires Member States to ensure that their national telecommunications administrations give their customers the opportunity to terminate long-term leasing contracts — concluded when the administrations held exclusive rights — to enable consumers to obtain supplies elsewhere if they wish. The directive is currently the subject of an action brought by France which claims that the Court of Justice should declare a number of its provisions void (OJ C 216, 18.8.1988, p. 6).

The European Commission took a further step in the creation of a single European market in telecommunications in 1989 in adopting on 26 June a directive under Article 90 of the Treaty of Rome which will allow independent undertakings to compete with the member states' telecommunications monopolies in offering new services on the telecoms network.

The Commission has decided that the new Article 90 directive will be notified to member states and so come into force when the Council finally adopts the Open Network Provision (ONP). The Article 90 directive will remove from the telecommunications authorities the complete monopoly to provide services which they currently enjoy in most member states. The telecommunications network itself, however, will not be touched by the Commission decision. This consists of the traditional telephone lines, fibre optic lines, micro-wave and satellite links, radio telephony and television cable networks; each member state is free to designate these as the sole responsibility of the existing telecoms authorities.

The telecoms monopolies can also be given exclusive rights to operate voice telephony, even after the ISDN (Integrated Services Digital Network) comes into operation. However, the national monopolies will no longer have responsibility for licensing private undertakings to use their networks.

In order to allow time for the telecommunications authorities to adapt to change, the resale of leased line capacity will not become subject to the directive until 1 January 1993.

A directive of this kind is an implementation of the law. Article 90 lays down rules for undertakings which have special and exclusive rights or are entrusted with operating services of "general economic interest" (such as post and telecommunications). While accepting certain limitations to the rules of competition, the Article states that the development of trade "must not be affected to such an extent as would be contrary to the interests of the Community".

As far as telecoms services are concerned, the Commission accepts that the provision of the basic telecoms network is of general economic interest. It also accepts that voice telephony — which accounts for 90 per cent of current telecoms business — should be protected. The provision of other services cannot be covered by this description, however, and should not be subject to the exclusive control of the national monopolies.

The basic requirements of the directive are as follows:

— Abolition of exclusive rights for all services to the general public except voice telephony — but member states may make such services subject to objective and non-discriminatory commercial regulations;

— Special transitional arrangements up to 31 December 1992, allowing a prohibition on the resale of leased line capacity which could then be used to compete with the public data-communication service before tariff structures have been revised;

- — Mandatory publication by member states of technical interfaces by 31 December 1990, so providing the information necessary for private operators;
- — Abolition of all restrictions on the processing of signals before and after their transmission via the public network;
- — Separation of regulatory powers from the activities of telecoms organisations;
- — Measures to allow existing long-term contracts to be terminated.

Banking and Financial Services

Australia

In 1987-88 a major Government Review of regulation of the financial services sector was undertaken following on from the significant deregulatory measures of the early to mid 1980s. The Review concentrated on those regulations which may cause inefficiencies both within and across different groups of financial institutions. The outcome of the Review is that further deregulation is not appropriate at present as financial markets are still adjusting to the rapid degree of change resulting from increased competition, technological developments and the internationalisation of the financial system.

Austria

Interbank agreements on interest rates (for savings deposits except for savings accounts at the base rate, savings certificates, savings with bonuses, sight deposits, private loans, current account overdrafts, loans, cash deposits, discount credit) expired on 30 June 1989. Thus it is expected that interest rates will be determined by market forces henceforth.

In addition, controls on capital movements have been liberalised, particularly in relation to long term foreign investment.

Belgium

There has been some deregulation of financial institutions notably as regards the removal of restrictions on the operations undertaken by the different types of financial institution, particularly banks and savings banks. The Act of 27 July 1985 modified the laws governing financial institutions in line with Community law and relaxed the monopoly that the banks and savings banks had on the use of the terms "bank" and "savings bank".

The Stock Exchange will soon be subject to a radical reform, the aim of which is to strengthen competition by opening up entry to financial markets by means of stock exchange companies and to make the Brussels financial market more attractive by allowing the emergence of organised new markets.

Canada

Deregulatory efforts in Canadian financial markets continue to present conflicts between federal-provincial and inter-provincial levels of government. In December 1988, the provincial finance ministers agreed to attempt resolution of some of the inter-provincial conflicts that have emerged from efforts to remove the traditional barriers to ownership between the four conventional "pillars" of the financial sector.

A new policy governing federally regulated financial institutions was announced in December 1986, and important sections of the legislation were enacted in July 1987. The policy updates the regulatory framework for Canadian financial institutions to permit more effective competition in domestic and foreign markets and improve protection to depositors, policyholders, and other creditors of federal institutions. A third piece of draft legislation addressing trusts and loans was released for discussion purposes on 21 December 1987.

The Department of Finance has suggested that draft legislation for the banking, trust, and insurance industries will be released in the new future, in order to relieve some of the conflicts and problems that now exist in financial markets across Canada.

Denmark

Banking

By Statute No. 306 of 16 May 1990, 4 EC Directives have been implemented in Danish banking law (the 2nd Bank Coordinating Directive, the Solvency Directive, the Equity Capital Directive, and the Annual Accounts Directive). The main features of the directives are:

— Common principles of mutual recognition and national control of the rules on initial capital and acquisition of holdings in other enterprises.

— Transfer of the required solvency from liabilities to assets and scaling down of the solvency ratio from 10 to 8 per cent with a concurrent scaling down and discontinuance in 1996 of inclusion of the base capital.

— Definition of liabilities being the total of the capital funds and additional capital.

— Access to insurance and mortgage-credit business as a subsidiary company and access to other types of business accessory to banking activities.

The directives are minimum directives which have been utilized in Danish law when fixing the solvency ratio. The national control implies that the competent authorities are responsible for supervision of the activities of domestic financial institutions in other countries. The implementation of the directives brings about an equality of the conditions for banking institutions within the EC as regards legislation and control, and consequently it provides the basis for more international competition.

In recent years the Danish banking sector has been influenced by several mergers. A temporary culmination of these trends was reached when two megabanks (Den Danske Bank and Unibank) were established, with effect from 1 January 1990, each as a consequence of mergers between three nationwide banking institutions. Each of the two

102

megabanks covers about 30 per cent of the total capital employed in Danish banks. The mergers were effected with the purpose of making the firms more competitive in relation to foreign banks.

Insurance business

As regards the insurance sector, a number of amendments were made in 1990 to the existing law in that field, such as a new Act on exchange of benefits in connection with insurance against loss or damage. The new legislation aims at implementing the 2nd EC Directive on insurance against loss or damage as a contribution to the harmonization of the insurance law within the EC.

There have only been a limited number of mergers within the insurance sector in recent years, as several mergers took place during the 1970s and 80s. The latest large-scale mergers were in 1988/89 when six insurance companies entered into three mergers. In 1990 two insurance companies made a declaration of intended merger, and another insurance company is contemplating merging with a bank. This is based on the wish to establish financial conglomerates, which from several quarters have been emphasized as a necessity within the financial sector.

Most large insurance companies in Denmark have started actual banking activities or have taken over existing banks.

Mortgage-credit business

In December 1989 a new Mortgage Credit Act entered into effect in order to implement the EC Mortgage Credit Directive and thus harmonize the legislation in that field, particularly as regards required reserves and access to the market.

Previously there had been quite a number of mergers within this sector, and in recent years the mortgage-credit institutes have established co-operation with the real estate business, for example by setting up chains of real estate agents on a franchise basis.

Banks, insurance companies and mortgage-credit institutes used to be within the jurisdiction of different authorities, but as from 1st January 1990, when the new Competition Act came into force, the authority in relation to the activities of banks, insurance companies as well as mortgage-credit institutes was vested in the Competition Council.

Finland

In recent years there has been some deregulation of financial markets, e.g. the regulation of interest rates was abolished in 1986.

The new Act on Restrictive Business Practices brings banking and insurance companies within its scope. In accordance with the law the supervision of competition in these fields is carried out jointly by the competition authorities and the specific authorities.

The banking legislation is undergoing changes. These will concern e.g. raising the reserve requirements of banks.

The Ministry of Social Affairs and Health in Finland has fixed the conditions and rates of the statutory insurance and also of some other insurance. In addition, on behalf of the Central Union of the Insurance Companies, there has been extensive co-operation. Because of the new Act on Restrictive Business Practices this co-operation is being dissolved. The law concerning foreign insurance companies is being changed.

France

The deregulation of the French financial system continued during the period 1985-1988.

The major reform consisted of breaking down the barriers in the capital market. Traditionally, this market was characterised by the existence of solid barriers between the money market (short term) and the financial market (medium and long-term). Access to each compartment was restricted to certain agents: in particular, individual persons and enterprises were not admitted to the money market.

The opening-up of the money markets proceeded by stages during the period 1985-1986:

1) The creation of negotiable certificates of deposit: banks were allowed to borrow on the short-term securities market which was open to all investors. The certificates of deposit are issued to a value of 5 million FF for a period of 6 months to 2 years;

2) Opening up of the money market (Act of 14 December 1985);

   a) Creation of commercial paper: this is paper issued by firms which offer sufficient guarantees to subscribers allowing direct access to the market without passing through a banking intermediary. Originally with a face value of FF 5 million, this was reduced to FF 1 million in 1988 to allow their use by smaller firms;

   b) Making Treasury bills available to individuals and firms. The denomination was fixed at 5 million with a 10-day minimum period;

   c) Specialised financial institutions were allowed to issue bonds, the objective being to allow such institutions to obtain short-term finance;

   d) Access to the interbank market has been restricted to financial institutions only: no longer will SNCF, insurance and social security establishments, pension funds and brokers' associations have access to this market;

   e) The Bank of France becomes the sole authority regulating the unified capital market;

3) Creation of a financial futures market. A 1987 Act brought commodities futures markets under the same authority as the financial futures market so that brokers approved by the Commodities Futures Commission can have access to the financial market and vice versa;

4) Creation of a negotiable share options market. This market permits hedging against share price fluctuations.

Paris financial markets were substantially modernised in response to growth in the markets. Thus:

1) New bond market instruments were created: single-coupon bonds, payable at final maturity and the splitting up of bonds to allow separate quotation of interest and capital payments.

2) The growth of jobbing firms — a Decree of 12 December 1985 defined the rules applicable to the establishment and statutes of jobbing firms.

3) The abolition of exchange control. Exchange control regulations for both individuals and firms have been totally abolished in recent years.

Modernisation of the Stock Exchange

An Act of 22 January 1988 has abolished the profession of broker and replaced it by brokerage firms which may be formed by firms outside the Stock Exchange. The Stock Exchange Council has taken over the function of establishing rules for the functioning of the market as well as disciplinary powers over the firms. A specialised institution — the French Stock Exchange Society (Société des bourses françaises) — has the role of looking after the day-to-day functioning of the market.

Monetary regulation has been changed so that fewer obligations are imposed on the banks.

As of the end of 1987, the banks are no longer required to have mandatory reserves in proportion to total loans. These reserve requirements have been replaced by an increase in mandatory reserves on deposits held which do not affect the rationing of credit.

Interest rates now regulate bank liquidity. The interbank market rate may now fluctuate more freely around the rates set by the Bank of France.

A number of technical changes relating to the intervention of the Bank of France have been made to encourage the operation of market forces.

Germany

In Germany, competition law exempted banking and insurance from the general ban against horizontal and vertical price agreements but subjected them to control to counteract potential abuse of this privilege. With the fifth law amending the Cartel Act, banks and insurance companies have been made subject to the ban. Patterned after the EC's prohibition of cartels, the grounds for exemptions apply only for cooperative arrangements that enhance or sustain performance and for pricing and setting contract terms if these activities improve demand satisfaction. All restrictions on competition remain fully subject to the provisions governing market-dominating enterprises and mergers.

The Deutsche-Verkehrs-Kredit-Bank has recently been privatised.

Ireland

Banks have expanded their range of activities into new areas such as life insurance and stockbroking. Building societies under recent legislation will be allowed to expand their range of activities into new areas such as unsecured lending, wider funding activities and other financial services. This will result in the future in greater competition between banks and building societies.

Japan

In Japan, a number of deregulatory measures have been enacted in recent years. In 1985 large time deposits (over 1 billion yen) and money market certificates were established at decontrolled interest rates. Subsequently the minimum amount of deposit has been reduced and the terms of issue liberalised. In June 1989 the small denomination money market certificate (minimum: 3 million yen) was introduced.

New Zealand

In the period leading up to the reforms of 1984-85, the New Zealand financial sector was heavily regulated. Financial markets were highly compartmentalised, with entry being generally very restrictive. The regulations allowed profits to be made fairly effortlessly, and risk was limited through industry protection and subsidies. The government was also heavily involved in the sector through ownership of some major financial institutions, including the Bank of New Zealand, the Rural Banking and Finance Corporation, the Development Finance Corporation, and the Post Office Savings Bank. In this environment, the scope for competition was limited — and there was little need for prudential supervision.

In 1984 the government moved to deregulate the financial sector and provide for greater competition and increased efficiency. In the nine months following mid-1984, interest rate and credit controls were abolished, compulsory investment ratios on financial institutions removed, exchange controls lifted, and the currency floated. From 1987 provision was made to register new banks — entry was open, but subject to some qualitative constraints. Competition in the financial sector generally was placed on a neutral basis by removing the discriminatory regulations which drew lines between different kinds of institutions and markets. Concurrently, the government moved to privatise the financial institutions it owned (although in the case of the BNZ this privatisation was only partial — the government still retains a majority shareholding).

In making these moves, the government recognised that the financial sector played a sufficiently central role in the economy to deserve the attention of the central authorities. Accordingly, at the same time as the changes in 1987 were made, a new prudential supervision framework was put in place in order to promote the maintenance of a sound and efficient financial system. This framework included, inter alia, a registration regime for monitoring banks, prudential monitoring of banks and some other large financial institutions, and the development of arrangements for managing the failure of any of those institutions, should that occur. More recently, following the enactment of a new Reserve Bank Act in 1989, the system of Reserve Bank prudential supervision was modified, in that supervision of large non-bank financial institutions ceased (most having become registered banks), and the supervisory approach was strengthened in certain respects. These arrangements are designed to make for a safer financial system. But they do not include insurance or other protections for bank depositors.

Norway

In 1988 the deregulation of the financial sector continued.

In the insurance market new legislation was introduced with a view to stimulating competition between insurance companies by a more liberal system of licensing. The permission for foreign non-life companies to do business in Norway has been extended to include all industry activities.

A new Act on financial services and financial institutions was passed. The new legislation is meant to stimulate efficiency by promoting competition between the different financial institutions.

A number of direct controls on the credit market were lifted. Bond financing of housing, power generating and primary industry is no longer under quota regulation.

Portugal

Banking has undergone considerable regulatory reform over the last 15 years. Since 1983, banking has been opened up to private enterprises, and since Portugal's adhesion to the European Community and the consequent commitments entered into in the light of European integration, several new private banks have been set up in Portugal, many of them resulting from the transformation of already existing investment companies. At the same time a currency exchange market functioned in 1985 and 1987 for spot exchange and forward exchange transactions. There has been a gradual liberalisation of international capital movements and especially since 1985, the Stock Exchange has been stimulated by the creation of Treasury bills and increase in the number of specialised new financial institutions. In addition, new financial instruments have been created with special financial assets taking the place of monetary assets.

Spain

A 1986 Royal Decree was issued which greatly facilitated access to the Spanish market by foreign banks by abolishing restrictions on the freedom to set up business. A calendar was established to allow complete integration of foreign banks in the system by 31 December 1992. A similar liberalisation has taken place in relation to insurance.

In 1987, a further Royal Decree established the rule that Community-based financial institutions would be subject to the same conditions as national institutions when wishing to establish a new financial institution in Spain, as from 1 January 1993.

The Royal Decree of 3 March 1987 removed all remaining State controls on interest rates on demand deposits, savings deposits and time deposits as well as on commissions related to loans by banks. However, in order to ensure transparency in financial markets, provisions requiring publicity of preferential rates, tariffs and conditions have been maintained as well as the obligation to provide customers with adequate information on transactions.

In 1988, the Act of 28 July laid down the regulations for the securities market with a National Securities Commission established to supervise the market. The Act is based on the principle of freedom to issue securities and on the free choice of investment instrument by the issuer. The Act established three official secondary markets — the Stock Exchanges, the Public Debt Market and any other secondary market designated by the government.

Another Act, of 29 July 1988, concerning the operation of control of credit institutions was adopted to regulate their operations and to ensure that they comply with government requirements, notably as regards their lending rates and own resources, as well as monitoring shareholdings in the institutions.

Another Royal Decree of 1988 concerned the creation of new banks and the establishment of foreign banks in Spain. The initial capital requirements for banks were increased and the entire amount of reserve capital must be paid at the time of the constitution of the bank. The Royal Decree also laid down provisions governing the creation of subsidiaries of foreign banks, in line with the Community rules.

The regulation of savings banks was also modified in 1988 allowing such banks to operate outside the region where they have their head office.

Sweden

In the banking area foreign banks have been allowed to establish themselves through subsidiaries since 1986. Recently a Committee has suggested that establishment through branches should also be permitted.

Moreover the whole credit market has undergone a broad investigation by a Committee, and continuous liberalisation during coming years can be expected as a result of this. However, certain new regulations can also be expected. Thus the Committee suggests that ownership of banks should be restricted. New legislation concerning finance houses (finansbolag) has come into force i.e. containing rules for authorisation.

Gradual abolition of the currency regulations has taken place during recent years. According to the government's budget proposal the aim is to abolish the regulation completely. Currency regulation will be preserved only for use in an emergency situation.

A broad investigation of the insurance industry by a Committee has also continued. Both liberalisation and certain new regulations can be expected as a result of this. This Committee suggests inter alia that the ownership of insurance companies should be limited. New legislation concerning insurance brokers gives the latter considerably better opportunities to do business in the Swedish market. Brokers have been rare so far. Brokers will also be able to act in Sweden as intermediaries for foreign insurance companies without needing a licence.

Switzerland

In 1988 the Swiss National Bank liberalised the rules governing the export of capital. Since then, there has been a general authorisation for loans denominated in Swiss francs as well as for currency swaps, when one of the parties is domiciled abroad. Moreover the rules for the quotation of securities on the Stock Exchange were relaxed.

A 1988 recommendation of the Swiss Cartels Commission put an end to the cartel affecting conditions in the property insurance market.

In April 1989, the Swiss Cartels Commission published a report entitled "The nationwide effects of inter-bank agreements". This report analyses 19 agreements and recommends their abolition or revision. The banks accepted 10 recommendations, and in five cases, the Cartels Commission considered the remedial measures proposed by the financial institutions to be satisfactory. Four recommendations — abolition of the uniform fees for custodian operations, of the brokerage agreement, of the syndicate of big banks concerning the underwriting of foreign-issued public bonds denominated in Swiss francs and the agreement on documentary credits — were rejected. The Minister of the Economy has decided to impose these four recommendations on the banks. The banks appealed against the imposition of the recommendation concerning custodian operations. Among the recommendations accepted by the banks mention should be made of: abolition of the granting of commission on public bond issues; abolition of the "Big Syndicate" on Swiss public debt issues; abolition of the common charges for cashing cheques; better accounting procedure for operations to avoid loss of days of interest; abolition of the agreement on long-term deposits in Swiss francs; abolition of the currency market agreement fixing the conditions for exchange into other currencies.

United Kingdom

The Stock Exchange

On 27 October 1986 the International Stock Exchange introduced its "Big Bang" reforms. These involved the replacement of the traditional single capacity system of brokers and jobbers by dual capacity market makers and broker dealers. The scale of fixed minimum commissions was abolished. The criteria for membership of the Exchange were revised over the period up to and including Big Bang to allow for the participation of outside firms. To support the changes a new screen-based quotation system was introduced from the same date.

The Financial Services Act 1986

The principal provisions of the Financial Services Act were brought into force on 29 April 1988. The regulatory system established under the Act is designed to work flexibly. It extends the previous legislation by broadening the scope to bring in additional investments and additional activities; by giving a more formal structure for regulating firms which belong to self-regulating organisations; by giving a wider range of powers to investigate and deal with misconduct by investment firms, and for investors to obtain redress; and by allowing the central function of setting standards and recognising the self-regulating organisations etc. to be transferred to the Designated Agency, the Securities and Investments Board (SIB).

Under the Act the Director General of Fair Trading is required to examine the rules, regulations, guidance and arrangements made by the various regulatory organisations established under the provisions of the Act and to report to the Secretary of State his opinion on whether their effect is to restrict, distort or prevent competition to any significant effect, or is intended or likely to do so. SIB could not be designated, nor other organisations recognised, until the Secretary of State had considered the Director General's reports and decided whether their rules had any significant anticompetitive effects, and if so, whether they were justified on investor protection grounds. The Director General made 26 reports to the Secretary of State before the new regulatory regime came into effect. He has a continuing duty to scrutinise the rules of SIB and the regulatory bodies with regard to their effect on competition and, since April 1988, he has made a number of reports further to this on-going responsibility. These include: the disclosure of information about life insurance products and commissions paid to independent financial advisers; and dissemination of company news and trade publication and price transparency on the International Stock Exchange.

The Building Societies Act 1986

This Act substantially broadens the range of financial and related activities in which building societies are permitted to engage. Previously, building societies were restricted to raising savings to on-lend on mortgage while the banks were constrained in the name of monetary policy in their ability to make loans and take deposits. During the 1970s and early 1980s a series of measures were taken to allow banks to compete with the building societies, notably to allow them to enter the mortgage market. The building societies retaliated by attempting to enter other financial markets. The 1986 Act extended these activities, notably by allowing the societies to have up to 5 per cent of their commercial assets in unsecured loans enabling them to offer a broad range of money transmission services, ownership of land and property for residential purposes and certain other assets. Although 90 per cent of their assets must be in the form of first mortgage loans on residential property, the societies may now offer other financial services such as pensions and insurance plans.

United States

In the banking sector, the Division filed comments in 1986 with the Federal Reserve Board, the Federal Deposit Insurance Corporation and the Comptroller of the Currency concerning a proposal to replace the current minimal capital requirements for member banks with a risk-based standard. Risk-adjusted capital requirements would force high-risk banks to maintain a large capital buffer, thereby reducing the likelihood that the deposit insurance fund would sustain losses when a bank performed poorly. By prohibiting banks from making certain capital structure and investment decisions, risk-adjusted capital requirements could prevent banks from taking advantage of valuable opportunities, the Division suggested. The Division urged the adoption of risk-adjusted deposit insurance premiums as an alternative. Their use would provide a market-oriented approach, the Division argued, by making high-risk banks bear the costs to the deposit insurance system in the form of higher insurance premiums. Risk-based capital requirements were adopted by the three banking agencies in early 1989, to be phased in completely by the end of 1992. Risk-based capital requirements were also imposed on savings associations in regulations promulgated in November 1989 by the Office of Thrift Supervision. None of the financial regulatory agencies, however, has adopted risk-adjusted premiums for deposit insurance.

In the area of securities regulation, the Division filed comments with the Securities and Exchange Commission ("SEC") opposing an SEC proposal to limit the ability of third parties to acquire stock during and following tender offers. (A tender offer is a public offer to purchase a specified amount of a company's stock, usually for purposes of gaining control of the company.) The SEC proposed the new rules in reaction to perceived abuses by entities that bought stock immediately after the withdrawal of tender offers. In general, the SEC's proposed rules would have required third parties who acquire 10 per cent or more of the shares subject to a tender offer to abide by the same rules as the firm making the tender offer. The SEC's proposal would also have extended the rules governing the behaviour of firms making tender offers for 30 days after the discontinuance of a tender offer.

In its comments to the SEC, the Division argued that the proposed rules would substantially harm the target corporation's shareholders by raising the cost of arbitrage purchases, particularly by limiting the opportunities of arbitrageurs to purchase and resell the stock of the target company to another firm seeking to gain control of that company. Because arbitrageur demand for the stock of tender offer targets would decline, the Division observed, the price of the target company's stock would reflect such lowered demand. Thus, the result of the SEC's proposed rules would be to disadvantage those takeover target shareholders who desired to avoid the risk that a takeover attempt would fail by selling to arbitrageurs. Moreover, the Division said, the new regulations had not been shown to provide any significant social benefits. By contrast, the proposed rules would interfere with the efficient and rational operation of the market for securities, the Division argued. At year's end, the SEC had not taken action on its proposed rules.

In the area of banking regulation, the Department filed comments in 1988 with the Federal Reserve Board concerning whether the Board should modify its general prohibition on acquisition and operation of thrift institutions (such as savings and loan associations) by bank holding companies. The Department argued that bank holding company acquisition and operation of thrift institutions should be generally authorised. In the Department's view, such a policy would produce significant benefits to the public by enhancing the financial stability and competitive vigour of the thrift industry, and by providing the managerial expertise necessary to encourage thrifts more fully to compete in the markets that had been opened to them by deregulatory legislation in the past eight years. The Department's comments also pointed out that widespread interstate banking and the trend toward nationwide expansion for depository institution holding companies should substantially mitigate any competitive or other concerns regarding interstate bank/thrift affiliations, particularly since geographic diversification by such holding companies would promote the soundness of depository institutions. The acquisition of thrift institutions by bank holding companies was authorised by the Federal Reserve Board in 1989, after the enactment of the Financial Institutions Reform, Recovery and Enforcement Act of 1989 expressly authorised the Federal Reserve Board to approve such acquisitions.

EEC

The Commission has consistently maintained that the competition rules are applicable in the banking sector in the same way as in other sectors of the economy, a policy upheld by the Court of Justice in the Züchner case (Case 172/83 Züchner v. Bayerische Vereinsbank AG (1981) ECR 2021). The Commission's decision of 10 December 1984 to exempt agreements on the international use and clearing of uniform Eurocheques under Article 85(3) was its first formal decision in the banking sector (Decision of 10.12.84, OJ L 35, 7.2.85. Fourteenth Competition Report, points 77-79). Four decisions adopted in the course of 1986 and one in 1989 break new ground in that they determined the compatibility of an entire range of agreements concluded within national banking associations of Member States with the competition rules. None of the decisions was concerned with interest rates: the Commission has decided to reserve its position on this matter. In the meantime, at the end of 1989, the Commission issued a press release [IP(89)869 of 16 November 1989] stating that such agreements on interest rates restricted competition and calling for their termination.

Irish banks

The Commission decided (Decision of 30.9.86, OJ L 295, 18.10.86) that a number of agreements between members of the Irish Banks Standing Committee (IBSC) did not appreciably restrict competition in the common market within the meaning of Article 85(1) and therefore granted them a negative clearance. The banks are the Allied Irish Banks plc, Bank of Ireland, Northern Bank Ltd and Ulster Bank Ltd. They are generally known as the associated Banks and are the main clearing and retail banks in Ireland. The agreements relate to common opening hours, clearing rules and a direct debiting system. Previous agreements relating to commissions for services to customers had already been voluntarily abandoned by the Associated Banks following a Community-wide investigation by the Commission into such agreements in the banking sector.

Belgische vereniging der banken/Association belge des banques

Following Commission intervention, a wide range of restrictive practices in the Belgian banking sector were abandoned. At the same time, the Commission exempted (Decision of 11/12/86, OJ L 7, 9.1.87) under Article 85(3) three agreements which were notified to it by the Belgian association of banks (Belgische vereniging der banken/ Association belge des banques BVB/ABB) — because they were beneficial to the fluidity of transactions in the banking sector.

The Commission found that the three agreements restricted competition within the meaning of Article 85(1) for the following reasons: two of them (the agreement on securities dealings and the one on international payments in foreign currencies or originating abroad) contained provisions concerning, respectively, the actual amount of the rebates, and of the commissions charged for acting as intermediary in these operations. As regards the third agreement (which concerns the collection of cheques and commercial bills originating abroad), its restrictive provisions consist in laying down the principle of charging a commission and the procedure for doing so.

Nevertheless, these three agreements were exempted, in particular because they contributed to an appreciable improvement of the services provided to customers and because the commissions are only maxima and not necessarily charged to customers.

The Commission attached an obligation to the decision: the BVB//ABB was required to inform the Commission immediately of any addition or amendment to the three agreements in question and of any new agreement concluded between its members within the Association. The exemption applies for ten years from 30 May 1986, the date of notification of the final version of the three agreements.

Associazione bancaria italiana

The Associazione Bancaria Italiana (ABI) is a non-profit-making association of all banks and other financial institutions established in Italy. In 1984 it notified 15 agreements and recommendations to the Commission. Five of these were subsequently abandoned following the Commission intervention. Of the remaining ten, seven have been declared not to restrict competition to an appreciable extent and thus not to violate Article 85(1); the remaining three, although restrictive of competition, were granted an exemption under Article 85(3) (Decision of 12.12.86, OJ L 43, 13.12.87; Bull. EC 12-1986, point 2.1.97).

With respect to those agreements granted negative clearance, one was concerned with technical matters only, whilst four dealt with the standardisation and rationalisation of banking operations on a national level, a matter which concerned operations in Italy only and hence did not appreciably affect trade between Member States. Two more agreements on minimum charges for safe deposits, although restrictive of competition, could not, in the Commission's view, be deemed to have an appreciable effect on trade.

Three agreements relating to the collection and acceptance of Italian bills and documents, the collection of cheques and assimilated instruments, and an interbank agreement on a new uniform type of lire travellers' cheque were considered by the Commission to be contrary to Article 85(1) in that they eliminated the freedom of members of the ABI to determine individually charges for banking services, thereby restricting competition between banking institutions and limiting consumer choice. Trade between Member States was affected since the agreements extended to foreign operations. Consequently although the agreements were clearly within the scope of Article 85(1), the Commission found that the conditions for the granting of an exemption under Article 85(3) were fulfilled. The agreements achieved the necessary standardisation and rationalisation of banking and credit services. As a result, a more efficient service at a reasonable cost could be provided. The fixing of a uniform rate for services was essential for the collaboration between banks and centralised clearing. Moreover, the agreements in question did not concern relations between banks and their customers, the extent to which the value date and commissions are passed on to customers being left to the discretion of the banks. They, therefore, constituted only one element of the final cost of the service provided to customers.

The exemption was granted for a period of ten years from the date of notification and was made subject to the obligation of the ABI to inform the Commission immediately of any changes in the commissions and value dates indicated in the notified agreements and of any new agreement concluded between the members of the association.

Dutch banks

In 1989, the Commission took a fourth decision on agreements within a national banking association (Decision of 19th July 1989, OJ L 253, 30.8.1989). As a result of this, several associations of Dutch banks abandoned in 1988 and 1989 a series of agreements providing in particular for:

— Uniform minimum commissions for several banking services between banks and to private and business customers;

— Uniform value dates for debit and credit operations;

— Uniform exchange rates and margins for foreign currency transactions;

— Uniform commissions and exclusive arrangements for foreign currency brokers in relation to certain financial services.

The Commission had objected that the agreements restricted competition and could not be exempted under Article 85(3), notably because they limited the scope for the banks concerned to develop their own commercial and financial policy independently and because they were discriminatory in that they required different charges to be made in certain situations for similar banking services.

The Commission Decision in this case states that a number of technical agreements which remained in force did not come under Article 85(1), either because they do not, or not appreciably, restrict competition, or because they do not appreciably affect trade between Member States.

The Decision also granted exemption under Article 85(3) to two circulars concerning simplified clearing procedures for cheques denominated in guilders or foreign currencies.

However, the Decision does not provide for any exemption for agreements on banking commissions. As regards agreements on commissions for services to clients, the Decision confirms the Commission's position in earlier Decisions, namely that agreements on commissions for services between banks may be exempted only in exceptional cases where they are really necessary for the successful implementation of certain forms of cooperation between several banks. This was not the case with the amended agreements as proposed by the parties.

The London Grain Futures Market; The London Potato Futures Association Limited; The London Meat Futures Exchange Limited; The GAFTA Soya Bean Meal Futures Association Limited; The International Petroleum Exchange of London Limited and the Baltic International Freight Futures Exchange Limited

The five decisions (Decisions of 10.12.86, OJ L 19, 21.1.87 and 4.12.86, OJ L 3, 6.1.87) relating to the Rules and Regulations of the above-mentioned terminal markets follow the previous decisions taken by the Commission with respect to the commodity markets in 1985.

Under the original Rules and Regulations as notified to the Commission, a fixed minimum commission for transactions carried out on the "floor" of the market was applicable. Furthermore, the rules on membership did not contain clear and objective criteria to be fulfilled by applicants for membership, making the markets so-called "closed shops".

As a result of the Commission's intervention the following amendments have been made to the Rules and Regulations:

i)   The references to the system of fixed minimum commission rates have been deleted; the rates of commission are now freely negotiable;

ii) The membership rules have been altered; membership is now regulated on the basis of objective criteria. In the interest of the protection of the rights of actual or potential members, an appeal procedure has been introduced.

Under these circumstances the Commission felt able to grant negative clearance in all five cases. A further negative clearance was granted in 1987 to the rules and regulations of the Baltic International Freight Futures Exchange, which were in accordance with the principles laid down in the previous decisions.

Uniform Eurocheques

The Commission took a favourable view of the agreements governing the conditions and procedures for the approval of undertakings concerned with the production and finishing of Eurocheques and Eurocheque cards (Decision of 19.12.1988 OJ L 36, 08.02.1989 — to be distinguished from the 1984 Decision on the international use and clearing of uniform Eurocheques).

There are some 9 000 European credit institutions which provide their customers with cheques and cards, and these must be of uniform quality, incorporating security devices to protect them from forgery and counterfeiting. Under the agreements in question, banks are required to obtain their cheques and cards only from approved printers who are in turn required to obtain watermarked paper from approved paper manufacturers. They have the choice of finishing the "Eurocheque" products themselves or of giving the work to authorised firms. In view of the nature of the products or services provided and the security requirements involved, the Commission decided that the principle of centralised prior approval could give rise to no objection.

The situation was different, however, as regards the finishing of the products, since the designation of enterprises for this purpose was the responsibility of the national associations. The Commission considered that this decentralised procedure might result in some distortion of competition in view of the discretion given to the national associations in the application of the approval criteria.

Accordingly, the guidelines for the finishing of Eurocheques and Eurocheque cards were granted an exemption under Article 85(3), whilst a negative clearance was issued in respect of the guidelines for their production.

Radio and Television Broadcasting

Australia

Television

Two important statutes designed to achieve the Government's policy objectives of a restructured and more competitive television broadcasting industry were passed in June 1987. The first is the Broadcasting Amendment Act 1987. This Act seeks to achieve three strategic goals: firstly, to provide services in most regional areas comparable to those in capital cities, that is equalisation; secondly, to create larger more viable markets in regional Australia through the process of aggregation; and, thirdly, to encourage competition by preventing the extension of existing regional monopolies through restrictions on ownership in any given aggregated market.

The major means of achieving these goals is aggregation. In Australia, all regional markets had been served by only one commercial television station as opposed to three in the five mainland States. Furthermore, the distances between television markets in Australia are generally so great that there is little if any overlap between them. The process of aggregation involves amalgamating a market serviced by only one commercial broadcaster with two similarly serviced adjacent markets. By using transmitters to reach all areas of an expanded market, a broadcaster which previously had a commercial monopoly in its own market would, over time, be brought to compete in an expanded market with two other commercial television broadcasters. Television stations are currently making the necessary infrastructure investments to provide aggregated TV services.

The second statute is the Broadcasting (Ownership and Control) Act 1987. This Act amends the Broadcasting Act 1942 by repealing the old two-station rule governing the ownership of commercial television and replacing it with firstly, a 60 per cent reach rule which allows persons to hold prescribed interests in any number of commercial television licences so long as the combined population of their service areas does not exceed 60 per cent of the Australian population; and, secondly, limits on cross-ownership between television and newspapers and between television and radio within the service area of the related commercial television licence.

The two-station rule was inequitable in that it took no account of the variations in audience reach between small regional television markets and the audience reach of the capital city markets, particularly Sydney and Melbourne. The new 60 per cent reach rule was intended to redress structural imbalance in the commercial television industry promoted by the two-station rule, while allowing the economies of scale necessary for the production of high quality Australian television programmes and for restructuring of programmes under the equalisation scheme.

Cross-media ownership rules are an integral part of the legislation. Such rules were introduced in tandem with the 60 per cent reach rule in order to curb a major expansion in television by existing newspaper or radio interests which already have considerable influence over the formation of public opinion. Raising the national ownership limit without placing limits on cross-media ownership would produce an unacceptable level of media concentration in local television service areas. Cross-media ownership rules were therefore introduced in order to maintain competition and discourage concentration of media ownership in local markets. Such action would thus enhance public access to a diversity of viewpoints, sources of news, information and commentary.

In general, the cross-media ownership rules prevent a person from buying a television licence to serve an area in which that person, for example, already owned a licence for a monopoly commercial radio station or in which that person had a prescribed interest in a daily newspaper whose main circulation was in the same area. The only radio operators who are affected by the new rules are those in the monopoly markets. This is because the influence of those in metropolitan and multi-station regional markets is seen as less dominant.

Further developments include examination of the feasibility of expansion of services in the more competitive television environment involving the introduction of cable television and related subscription television services.

Radio

In October 1987, the government announced a major new package of commercial radio ownership rules that would provide an efficient and equitable framework for the future development of radio services in Australia.

The major change to the ownership rules involves an increase from eight to 16 in the permissible number of radio stations in which any one person can hold a prescribed interest, together with new limits on the number of radio licences a person can hold in each service area and in each State. The Broadcasting (Ownership and Control) Bill was introduced into Parliament in December 1987 to give effect to these changes, although it was subsequently revised and reintroduced in April 1988.

In conjunction with these new ownership rules, the Broadcasting Amendment (Ownership & Control) Bill 1987 imposed a new system of 'establishment fees' for new regional commercial radio licences. The scheme will ensure that new licensees make a fair contribution to the community from their commercial access to the broadcasting spectrum.

The introduction of the 60 per cent reach rule and the associated cross-media rules have seen major structural changes of ownership within the television industry and a diluting of cross-media holdings.

Recent developments in radio include the expansion of community radio services and wider opportunities for competition with the expansion of the spectrum from AM into FM.

Belgium

In Belgium, radio and television broadcasting is the responsibility of the local communities. In 1987, the Flemish-speaking communities created the possibility of introducing privately financed broadcasts. In January 1987 a decree was adopted enabling the operation of private television companies covering the entire Flemish community, private associations operating in a local or regional community, private associations aiming at broadcasting to a particular audience as well as private pay television channels. Thus the public broadcasting monopoly was broken up and several private companies have begun operations since 1987.

A similar process of deregulation has occurred in the French-speaking community.

Canada

The Canadian Radio-Television and Telecommunications Commission is intending to review cable regulations in 1989 with the aim of streamlining the regulatory process and lessening the regulatory burden on the cable industry.

Denmark

Following an amendment to the Act on radio and television broadcasting in June 1987, the independent institution TV2 was established in October 1988. TV2, which is partly financed through advertising, competes with the public institution Danmarks Radio, which is not allowed to use commercials.

Licences for local radio and television broadcasting are granted by regional boards for a fixed period — a maximum three years for radio and five years for television. The licence may be renewed at the end of the period.

In June 1990 a new consolidated Act on radio and television broadcasting was issued. The Act contains rules on the time allowed for commercial advertising which may not exceed 10 per cent of the total daily broadcasting time. This applies to TV2 as well as to the local radio and television channels.

The new Competition Act came into force on 1 January 1990. The Act applies to commercial enterprises and associations of such enterprises, including business activities performed by public authorities. A number of measures against harmful effects of anti-competitive practices do not apply, however, to such business activities which, under special provisions, are subject to control or approval by public authorities, including the radio and television channels. Such measures concern for instance orders to annul agreements and to fix maximum prices etc. But the Competition Council may approach the competent public authority and point to the potentially harmful effects on competition. Such communications are published.

France

The Acts of 30 September 1986 and 17 January 1989 relating to freedom of communication were decisive steps in the liberalisation of broadcasting in France. The traditional state monopoly was abandoned in favour of competition. Thus, all activities in the audiovisual communication field are open to private enterprise whether the establishment of broadcasting stations, their operation or use. The 1986 Act also provided for the privatisation of one television channel — TF1. The public sector still has a role however with two TV channels remaining under public ownership. In addition, the notion of public service remains embodied in the new regime which provides for a system of authorisations awarded by the Supreme Broadcasting Council (Conseil Supérieur de l'Audiovisuel), a new regulatory authority which was established by the Act of 17 January 1989.

There are two main principles governing the establishment and operation of enterprises in the sector: transparency and restriction on concentration of ownership. The firms must operate under their own name only and must make publicly available information on their structure and ownership. The Act prohibits control by one person of two national radio or television channels if their total audience exceeds 15 million people.

The Supreme Broadcasting Council is responsible for guaranteeing observance of these fundamental principles, in particular by encouraging free competition, ensuring equality of treatment, plurality of opinion and freedom of information.

The Council is empowered to issue licences to private operators which are valid for ten years for television services and five years for radio services. In the public sector, the Council also has wide monitoring powers and appoints the chairmen of the public companies.

Finland

Cable transmission is a rapidly increasing business in Finland. However, because only a few enterprises exist, competition is limited at present. The Law on Cable Transmission has been in force since 1 June 1987. Under the Law, the conditions of entry are regulated.

The Radio Law came into force on 1 October 1988. Trade in radio equipment was liberalised by the Law.

In Finland, there were 38 commercial local radio stations operating at the end of 1988. In addition, there were some non-commercial stations. The number of local stations is increasing.

Germany

In Germany, the process by which the Laender have been creating the legal basis for private broadcasting in recent years has been completed. The transition from exclusively public broadcasting systems to such as include private broadcasters has now been implemented in both the radio and television areas. While the main transmission medium for private television remains the cable, satellite and terrestrial transmission is visibly gaining ground. The Federal Cartel Office has reinforced the trend toward opening up broadcasting markets for private operators by rigorous application of the anti-trust laws, also in the area of competition-impeding exclusive contracts for publicly owned stations. It prohibited such a contract from being concluded with the Deutscher Sportbund for the broadcasting of popular events. The Federal Cartel office also prohibited a proposed joint venture between a regional public radio broadcaster (WDR) and the only competing private radio broadcaster on the grounds that the existing market dominating position of the public broadcaster in the advertising sector would be further strengthened. In addition, the federal government has worked hard to ensure to the greatest possible extent that the EC does not overdo regulations in this area. In particular, it has opposed an arrangement that would have ensured European programmes a minimum quota of radio and television broadcasting time.

Ireland

The Radio and Television Act, 1987 was enacted providing for new independent broadcasting services as follows:
— an independent national radio service,
— independent local radio services,
— neighbourhood and special interest radio stations,
— an independent national television service.

Prior to the enactment of the legislation broadcasting in Ireland was in the hands of RTE, the State broadcasting service. Since the end of 1988, franchises for the national radio service, the national television service and 23 local radio services have been handed out by an Independent Radio and Television Commission. Some of the successful franchises have commenced broadcasting.

New Zealand

In 1988 the state-owned Broadcasting Corporation was restructured into two companies: Radio New Zealand and Television New Zealand. At the same time TVNZ's monopoly on television broadcasting and a complex warrants system were abolished.

In 1989 more flexible provisions on foreign and cross-media ownership were introduced and advertising hours restrictions were liberalised. The government's social objectives for broadcasting are being met under a competitive grants scheme and through retained state ownership of two television channels and two radio networks.

It is expected that there will be increased demand for spectrum and scarcity in some frequencies. New legislation will be passed shortly whereby the allocation of management rights will be made on the basis of a sealed bid (second price) auction. Rights will be tradeable.

Norway

From 15 October 1988, when the legislation on the transmission of satellite TV programmes on cable came into force, a licence for such transmission has no longer been required. This means that any TV channel relayed by satellite that can be received in Norway will in principle be available to everyone who wants to see it.

Legislation on local broadcasting was passed on 1 May 1988 and liberalised the licensing of local radio and TV stations.

Portugal

Television broadcasting remains a State monopoly in Portugal, but the government intends to open up the sector to private enterprise.

However, some liberalisation has occurred in radio broadcasting since the adoption of Decree Law No 338 of 28 September 1988, which enables private operators to begin broadcasting if they satisfy basic requirements for the award of a licence.

Spain

Act 10/1988 of 3 May was designed to regulate the operation of private television stations, while retaining the principle that television broadcasting was an essential public service. Thus, the Act lays down the conditions for the award of licences to private firms, the duration of the licence, the content of the broadcasts (minimum length of broadcast time, advertising, programme origin) and the firms licensed (ownership by domestic and foreign individuals). The Act also prescribes a system of infringements and penalties. The Act fixes at three the number of licences to be awarded by the Council of Ministers and lays down the criteria for selecting among competing offers, with special attention being paid to safeguarding the plurality of ideas and opinions and the diversity of information.

Switzerland

Since 1985, regulatory reform has taken the form of greater liberalisation. Thus, the Order on local radio trials has been amended several times to allow more advertising on local radio stations. New trial authorisations have been issued in areas deprived of local radio. Instructions on television advertising also allow the Swiss Broadcasting Corporation (SSR) to increase advertising on its channels. The federal decree on satellite broadcasting which was adopted by Parliament recently permits the granting of franchises for international television programmes. It authorises all kinds of methods of financing transmissions and settles the question of exclusive rights. As regards the transmission of foreign programmes by Swiss cable networks, the temporary application of the Council of Europe Convention on transfrontier television has led to a relaxation of applicable criteria. The Teletext franchise has also been modified to allow a new form of financing the service. Finally, mention should be made of the federal radio and television bill at present before Parliament. This law would replace the regulations now in effect and scattered throughout various texts. It is designed to establish competition between private broadcasters at local and regional levels, and partially at national level. In addition, at national level and in the linguistic regions, it ensures that the Swiss Broadcasting Corporation has a preferential position, while allowing the establishment of other broadcasting companies, provided that the latter do not endanger the former's public service mission. The law pays special attention to the negative effects that may result from a dominant position in the media.

EEC

European Broadcasting Union

A number of members of the European Broadcasting Union had planned to group together to fix joint rates and conditions for the use of television news items taken from the network by third parties. Upon being advised by the Commission that this would restrict competition within the common market (Bull. EC 7/8-1986, point 2.1.61), in that intended purchasers would no longer be able to negotiate separately with individual broadcasters, the broadcasters abandoned their plans. They have reverted to their previous practice of negotiating separately with purchasers.

Appendix

Footnotes to Tables

Energy (Tables 1 - 3)

1. These tables cover the petroleum (meaning refined petroleum products as opposed to crude oil), natural gas and electricity sectors.

2. For these tables, *"regulated" entry* means controls which limit the number of firms. This could be, for example, through an explicit quota or through a requirement that the firm obtain a certificate of convenience and necessity, license or comparable document. *"Partly regulated" entry* applies to situations where some substantial liberalisation has occurred: for example, where a quota has been continued but the limit raised significantly or where the requirement of a license or certificate of convenience and necessity has been continued but the burden of proof has been shifted to incumbent firms to prove that the firm should not enter. *"Unregulated" entry* refers to situations where there was no cap or other limit on the number of firms. Requirements related to competence ("fit, willing and able"), safety, the environment, financial responsibility, etc. are not be counted as regulation for this table.

3. *"Regulated" prices* refers to situations where the firm's prices, fees or rates are set or approved by the regulatory authority. *"Partly regulated"* refers to situations where the firm is given some but not complete freedom in setting price. For example, a system of rate zones or permissible percentage changes would be partial regulation. Also included here are such new regimes as "RPI - X" and price cap policies as substitutes for price setting regulation. ("Price cap" refers to policies which set a maximum price but permit lower prices.) Include here as well rate of return regulation, as such regulation gives the firm some flexibility in setting price. *"Unregulated" prices* refers to situations where the firm has complete freedom in setting price. Also included here are systems which require the firm to file its prices or rates with a regulatory authority but that authority has no legal authority to challenge a fare as too high or too low. Also included here are the regimes which result in de facto deregulation of prices but retain the legal authority to regulate them, e.g. where prices or rates must be filed and approved by the regulatory authority and that authority is currently approving routinely any submitted fares. Fees levied by government, e.g. license fees, environmental charges, etc. have not been counted as regulation. Also not counted as regulation is the ability of the government to challenge prices under competition law.

4. The aspects of regulation treated are entry, service (for example, routes, backhaul restrictions, frequency) and prices.

5. In drafting the specifications for these tables, there was the view that regulation of entry was synonymous with regulation of service and that these two aspects should thus be combined into one response. In at least one country, however, the regulation of entry turns out to be distinct from service. Thus the tables include both. For countries which treat entry and service as one, the response is repeated for both categories.

6. For these tables, *"regulated" entry* means controls which limit the number of firms. This could be, for example, through an explicit quota or through a requirement that the firm obtain a certificate of convenience and necessity, license or comparable document. *"Partly regulated"* entry applies to situations where some substantial liberalisation has occurred. For example, where a quota has been continued but the limit raised significantly or where the requirement of a license or certificate of convenience and necessity has been continued but the burden of proof has been shifted to incumbent firms to prove that the firm should not enter. *"Unregulated" entry* refers to situations where there was no cap or other limit on the number of firms. Requirements that the firm be "fit, willing and able", i.e. requirements related to safety, competence, financial responsibility, etc. have not been counted as regulation for this table.

7. *"Regulated" prices* refers to situations where fares or rates are set or approved by the regulatory authority. *"Partly regulated"* refers to situations where the firm is given some but not complete freedom in setting price. For example, a system of rate zones or permissible percentage changes would be partial regulation. *"Unregulated" prices* refers to situations where the firm has complete freedom in setting price. Also included here are systems which require the firm to file its fares or tariffs with a regulatory authority but that authority has no legal authority to challenge a fare as too high or too low. Also included here are regimes which result in de facto deregulation of prices but retain the legal authority to regulate them, e.g. where prices or rates must be filed and approved by the regulatory authority and that authority is currently approving routinely any submitted fares. Fees levied by government, e.g. license fees, road user charges, landing fees, etc. have not been counted as regulation. Also not counted as regulation is the ability of the government to challenge prices under competition law.

8. *"Regulated" service* refers to situations where routes, capacity and scheduling are set or approved by the regulatory authority. *"Partly regulated"* refers to situations where the firm is given some but not complete freedom in selecting the services it offers. For example, a flexible system of capacity control would be partial regulation. *"Unregulated" service* refers to situations where the firm has complete freedom in choosing the services it offers. Also included here are systems which require the firm to file its routes with a regulatory authority but that authority has no legal authority to challenge that choice of service on economic grounds. However, authority to prohibit service for non-economic grounds such as environmental, safety or infrastructure reasons have not been counted as regulation, e.g.,

no service after a certain hour, no more than a certain number of landing slots at a given time, no trucks on a given road or bridge, etc. Also not counted as regulation is the ability of the government to challenge services under competition law.

Communications (Tables 10 - 14)

9. For these tables, *basic telephone service* is defined as service which is offered to the public generally and for which there are no obstacles due to technology, contractual terms or tariff restraints to communication between any two telephones on the system. In other words, this is a pure communications path which is transparent to the user. *Value-added or enhanced service* is more than basic service.

10. It is difficult to come up with a distinction between *local and long distance services* which will hold across countries. For example, some countries distinguish long distance service in part by the fact that long distance charges reflect call duration and local charges do not, but duration-based charges for local calls exist in other countries. Lacking a definition, countries were left to their own good judgement in making this distinction.

11. The distinction between *"Type I"* and *"Type II"* telephone service providers is made in the tables. Type I providers build their own network facilities while Type II firms lease lines from Type I firms. Countries which do not distinguish between the two types of providers were asked to make the same response for each type and add some explanatory text.

12. For *equipment* the focus is on equipment located on the customer's premises, e.g. PBXs, key systems and basic telephones. The tables exclude such things as the switching equipment located at the central office of the service provider or transmission equipment.

13. For these tables, *"regulated" entry* means controls which limit the number of firms. This could be, for example, through a prohibition on entry, an explicit quota or through a requirement that the firm obtain a certificate of convenience and necessity, license or comparable document. *"Partly regulated" entry* applies to situations where some substantial liberalisation has occurred. For example, where a quota has been continued but the limit raised significantly or where the requirement of a license or certificate of convenience and necessity has been continued but the burden of proof has been shifted to incumbent firms to prove that the firm should not enter. *"Unregulated" entry* refers to situations where there was no cap or other limit on the number of firms. Requirements related to competence (e.g. "fit, willing and able"), equipment compatibility, financial responsibility, etc. are not counted as regulation for this table.

14. *"Regulated" prices* refers to situations where the firm's prices, fees or rates are set or approved by the regulatory authority. *"Partly regulated"* refers to situations where the firm is given some but not complete freedom in setting price. For example, a system of rate zones or permissible percentage changes is treated as partial regulation. Also included here is rate of return regulation, as that regulation leaves the firm some flexibility in setting prices. Included here as well are such new

127

regimes as "RPI - X" and price cap policies as substitutes for price setting or rate of return regulation. Also included here are price minimums; such minimums may be applied to courrier services, for example, to protect the post office. *"Unregulated" prices* refers to situations where the firm has complete freedom in setting price. Included here as well are systems which require the firm to file its prices with a regulatory authority but that authority has no legal authority to challenge a price as too high or too low. Also included here are regimes which result in de facto deregulation of prices but retain the legal authority to regulate them, e.g. where prices or rates must be filed and approved by the regulatory authority and that authority is currently approving routinely any submitted fares. Fees levied by government, e.g. license fees, taxes on phone service, etc. are not counted as regulation. Also not counted as regulation is the ability of the government to challenge prices under competition law.

Extent of public ownership (Tables 4 - 6, 9, 15 - 17)

15. The public ownership category applies where a supplier is either fully or majority-owned by the government.

16. The "mixed" category includes situations where a publicly-owned firm is in competition with privately-owned firms or where the government has a minority stake in at least one of several firms in the market.

17. It was less obvious how to treat a minority public stake in a monopoly provider. For this situation delegates were asked to use their judgement in deciding whether the government's influence over the firm was sufficient to characterize it as publicly-owned.

18. As in the previous tables, these tables are limited to describing ownership at the federal level. Details as to ownership at the state or provincial level appear in the text.

Notes

1. Recommendation of the Council on Competition Policy and Exempted or Regulated Sectors of 25th September 1979 [C(79)155(Final)]. This Recommendation urged Member countries in particular: "to undertake, with the participation of competition authorities, reviews of regulatory regimes and of exemptions from restrictive business practices laws to consider:

    a) whether the initial reasons or circumstances which gave rise to regulations, or to particular aspects thereof, remain valid under contemporary conditions;

    b) the extent to which those regulatory regimes or particular aspects thereof have achieved their objectives, and the true social, economic and administrative costs, as compared to benefits, of achieving those objectives by means of regulation;

    c) whether the same objectives could in fact be achieved under contemporary conditions by the operation of competition subject to control under restrictive business practices laws, or by forms of government intervention which restrict competition to a lesser degree."

2. OECD (1979), *Competition Policy in Regulated Sectors*, Report of the Committee of Experts on Restrictive Business Practices, Paris.

3. See BAUMOL, W.J., J.C. Panzer and R.D. Willig (1982), *Contestable Markets and the Theory of Industry Structure*, Harcourt Brace Jovanovich (New York) for a discussion of the main issues in contestability theory.

4. KAY, J.A. and J. Vickers (1988), "Regulatory Reform in Britain", *Economic Policy*, pp. 321-323.

5. AVERCH, H. and L. Johnson (1962) "Behaviour of the Firm under Regulatory Constraint", *American Economic Review* 52: 1052-1069.

6. LITTLECHILD, S.C. (1983), *Regulation of British Telecommunications Profitability,* Department of Industry.

7. VICKERS, J. and G. Yarrow (1986), "Telecommunications: liberalisation and the privatisation of British Telecom", in J.A. Kay, C.P. Mayer and D.J. Thompson, *Privatisation and Regulation — the UK Experience*, Oxford University Press, Oxford.

8. MORRISON, H. (1933), *Socialisation of Transport*, HMSO.

9. MORRISON, H. (1933).

10. REES, R. (1984), "A positive theory of the public enterprise', in: M. Marchand, P. Pestieau and H. Tulkens (eds), *The Performance of Public Enterprises*, North Holland, Amsterdam.

11. See for a discussion of principal and agent applications to regulation, Kay, J. A. and J. Vickers (1988).

12. For a survey of recent contributions on regulatory failure/regulatory capture, see Sappington, D. and J.E. Stiglitz (1987), "Information and Regulation in E.E. Bailey (1987), *Public Regulation: New Perspectives on Institutions and Policies*, MIT Press, Cambridge.

13. OECD (1988), *Deregulation and Airline Competition*, Annex II, p. 103.

14. CHRISTIANSEN, G.B. and R.H. Haveman. (1981), "Public Regulation and the Slow Down in Productivity Growth", *American Economic Review* 76, pp. 559-63.

15. OECD (1986), *New Zealand's Report on Competition Policy and Deregulation*, Committee of Experts on Restrictive Business Practices, Working Party No. 2, Paris.

16. See PRYKE, R. (1981) *The Nationalised Industries; Policies and Performance since 1968*, Oxford; Martin Robertson for a discussion of the UK experience; and Monsen, J.R. and K.D. Walters (1983), *Nationalised Companies: A Threat to American Business*, McGraw-Hill, for a Europe-wide analysis.

17. PERA, A., 1989, "Deregulation and Privatisation in an Economy-wide Context", *OECD Economic Studies* No. 12, Spring, p. 170.

18. MCKIE, J.W. (1989), "US Regulatory Policy", in K.J. Button and D. Swann (eds), *The Age of Regulatory Reform*, Oxford.

19. STARKIE, D. (1989), "Deregulation: The Australian Experience", in K.J. Button and D. Swann (eds), *The Age of Regulatory Reform* (1989), Oxford.

20. BISHOP, M.R., and J.A. Kay (1988), *Does Privatisation Work? Lessons from the UK*, Centre for Business Strategy, London Business School.

21. STARKIE, D. (1989).

22. HALEY, J.O (1989), "The Context & Content of Regulatory Change in Japan", in K.J. Button and D. Swann (eds), *The Age of Regulatory Reform* (1989), Oxford.

23. D. STARKIE (1989).

24. Les Notes Bleues (1988), *Les Notes Bleues* no. 369, 1-7 February.

25. BISHOP, M.R. and J.A. Kay (1988).

26. LAWSON, N. (1987), reported in *The Observer*, 25 October 1987.

27. ENCAOUA, D., and J-J Santini (1987), *Les privatisations en France: Elements d'une politique libérale ?*, presented at the EIPA colloquium, "Privatisation in the European Communities: A Comparative Perspective", Maastricht.

28. US Department of Justice, Antitrust Division (1987), *The Geodesic Network: 1987 Report on Competition in the Telephone Industry* ("The Huber Report").

29. PERA, A. (1989), p. 161.

30. The following paragraphs are based on the replies from 15 Member countries — Australia, Austria, Canada, Denmark, Finland, Germany, Ireland, Japan, New

Zealand, Norway, Sweden, Switzerland, Turkey, the UK and the US — to a questionnaire on regulation and public ownerships (see Part II, Tables 1 to 17).

31. See MILLWARD, R. (1982), "The comparative performance of public and private enterprise", in: Lord Roll (ed.), *The Mixed Economy*, Macmillan, London.

32. BORCHERDING, T.E., et al. (1982), *Comparing the Efficiency of Private and Public Production: The Evidence from Five Countries*, Zeitschrift für Nationalökonomie, Supplementum 2.

33. MILLWARD, R. (1982).

34. BAILEY, E.E, (1986), "Price and productivity change following deregulation: the US experience", *Economic Journal*, vol. 96.

35. MORRISON, S. and C. Winston (1986), *The Economic Effects of Airline Deregulation*, Washington, D.C., Brookings Institution, pp. 25-33.

36. OECD (1986), *New Zealand's Report on Competition Policy and Deregulation*.

37. OECD (1988), *Structural Issues in the EDRC Country Reviews, 1988 Report by the Secretariat on Results by Subject Area*, Economic and Development Review Committee, Paris.

38. OECD (1986), *Competition Policy & Deregulation: Developments Since the Adoption of the 1979 Council Recommendation on Competition Policy and Exempted or Regulated Sectors*, Committee of Experts on Restrictive Business Practices, Paris; and OECD (1988), *Structural Issues in the EDRC Country Reviews, 1988 Report by the Secretariat on Results by Subject Area*.

39. OECD (1988) *Structural Issues in the EDRC Country Reviews, 1988 Report by the Secretariat on Results by Subject Area*.

40. See OECD (1989), *Competition Policy and the Deregulation of Road Transport*, Chapter 3, for further details.

41. MOORE, T. (1976), *Trucking Regulation: Lessons from Europe*, Washington, D.C.

42. OECD (1988), *Structural Issues in the EDRC Country Reviews, 1988 Report by the Secretariat on Results by Subject Area*.

43. DARDIES, R., J. Garkey, and Z. Zhang (1989), "Deregulation of Trucking in the United States — Implications for Consumers", *Journal of Consumer Policy*, Vol. 2, No., 1 March, p. 19.

44. OKANO, Y. (1989), *The Privatisation of the Japanese National Railways — The Early Experience*, paper presented at the joint ISEAS/EIPA conference, "Privatisation: Lessons from Europe & ASEAN", Singapore, February.

45. OECD (1987), *Structural Adjustment and Economic Performance*, Paris.

46. See Part II, p. 88.

47. See Part II, p. 93.

48. CAVES, D.W., and L.R. Christensen (1978), *The Relative Efficiency of Public and Private Firms in a Competitive Environment: the Case of Canadian Railroads*, Social Systems Research Institute, Workshop Series.

49. BISHOP, M.R. and J.A. Kay (1988).

50. DOMBERGER, S., S.A. Meadowcroft and D.P. Thompson (1986), "Competitive Tendering and Efficiency: the Case of Refuse Collection", *Fiscal Studies*, vol. 7, No. 4; and (1987), "The Impact of Competitive Tendering on the Costs of Hospital Domestic Services", *Fiscal Studies*, vol. 8, no. 4.

51. WERDEN, G.J., A.S. Joskow and R.L. Johnson (1989), *The Effects of Mergers on Economic Performance: Two Case Studies from the Airline Industry*, US Department of Justice Economic Analysis Group Discussion Paper. The study found that the merger of TWA and Ozark appeared to have caused a slight increase in fares and a far greater reduction in service on city pairs out of St. Louis, while the merger of Northwest and Republic appeared to have caused a significant increase in fares and a significant reduction in overall service on city pairs out of Minneapolis-St. Paul.

52. OECD (1988), *The Consumer Impact of Liberalisation and Regulatory Reform in the Field of Financial Services*, Note by the Secretariat, Committee on Consumer Policy, Paris.

53. Price Waterhouse (1988), *The Cost of non-Europe in Financial Services*.

54. OECD (1988), *The Consumer Impact of Liberalisation and Regulatory Reform in the Field of Financial Services*, ibid.

55. PRYKE, R. (1982), " The comparative performance of public and private enterprise," *Fiscal Studies,* vol. 3, no. 2.

56. PESCATRICE, D.R., and J.M. Trapani (1980), "The performance and objectives of public and private utilities operating in the United States", *Journal of Public Economics*, vol. 13, no. 2.

57. FINSINGER, J., and M.V. Pauly (eds, 1985), *The Economics of Insurance Regulation: A Cross-National Study*, Macmillan, London.

58. BISHOP, M.R. and J.A. Kay (1988), ibid.

59. BISHOP, M.R. and J.A. Kay (1988), Ibid.

60. DAVIS, E.H. (1984), "Express Coaching since 1980: Liberalisation in Practice", *Fiscal Studies*, vol. 5, no. 1.

61. JAFFER and THOMPSON (1986), "Deregulating Express Coaches: A Reassessment", *Fiscal Studies*, 1986.

62. LEVINE, M.E. (1987), "Airline Competition in Deregulated Markets: Theory, Firm Strategy, and Public Policy", *Yale Journal on Deregulation*.

63. PRYKE, R. (1982).

64. HAMMOND, E.M., D.R. Helm and D.J. Thompson (1986), "Competition in Electricity Supply has the Energy Act failed?", *Fiscal Studies*, vol. 7, no. 1.

65. VICKERS, J., and G. Yarrow (1988), *Privatisation—an Economic Analysis*, MIT Press, Cambridge.

66. See, for example, DEMSETS H. (1968) "Why Regulate Utilities?" *Journal of Law and Economics* 11:55-65; Domberger, S. (1989), *A Reconsideration of Franchise Contracts for Natural Monopolies*, paper presented to UN Department of Technical Co-operation for Development Interregional Seminar on Performance Improvement of Public Enterprises in Developing Countries, New Delhi, April

132

1989; Sharpe T. (1982), *The Control of Natural Monopoly by Franchising*, mimeo, Wolfson College, Oxford; Vickers, J. and G. Yarrow (1988), ibid; and Williamson O.E (1976), "Franchising Bidding for Natural Monopolies — In General and with Respect to CATV", *Bell Journal of Economics* 7:73-104.

67. SCHMALENSEE, R. (1979), *The Control of Natural Monopolies*, Lexington, Washington, D.C.

68. DOMBERGER, S. (1989), ibid.

69. BISHOP, M.R. and J.A. Kay (1988), ibid.

70. BRÖKER, G. (1989), *Competition in Banking*, OECD, Paris. See in particular Annexes I and IV.